W9-BYB-967

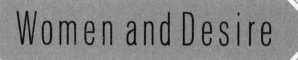
Women and Desire

POLLY YOUNG-EISENDRATH, PH.D.

Women and Desire

Beyond Wanting
to Be Wanted

HARMONY BOOKS   NEW YORK

Copyright © 1999 by Polly Young-Eisendrath

All rights reserved. No part of this book may be reproduced or transmitted in any form or by any means, electronic or mechanical, including photocopying, recording, or by any information storage and retrieval system, without permission in writing from the publisher.

Published by Harmony Books, 201 East 50th Street, New York, New York 10022. Member of the Crown Publishing Group.

Random House, Inc. New York, Toronto, London, Sydney, Auckland
www.randomhouse.com

Harmony Books is a registered trademark and Harmony Books colophon is a trademark of Random House, Inc.

Printed in the United States of America

Library of Congress Cataloging-in-Publication Data
Young-Eisendrath, Polly.
　　Women and desire : beyond wanting to be wanted / by Polly Young-Eisendrath. — 1st ed.
　　Includes bibliographical references and index.
　　1. Women—Psychology.　2. Desire.　I. Title.
　HQ1206.Y69 — 1999
　155.6'33—dc21   99-13426
                                                                   CIP

ISBN 0-609-60371-X
10　9　8　7　6　5　4　3　2　1
FIRST EDITION

Lovingly dedicated to Amber Rickert

and Heidi Yockey

Acknowledgments

MY FIRST GRATITUDE is to the women I have seen in psychoanalysis and psychotherapy, who have provided the basis for my study and understanding of female desire. The work I do is such a rare and great privilege. In what other profession would I be invited into the most personal, intimate, and vulnerable places of human life?

People who are not therapists frequently ask me about the fatigue or burnout that is assumed to accompany long hours of doing psychotherapy. I have little fatigue; I am inspired and energized by this work. My clients invite me daily to understand the roots of human suffering and the hope for its transformation. I become ever more optimistic about our capacities for change through conscious awareness. As my clients grow in awareness, compassion, and insight, I repeatedly witness the paths we all must follow from confusion about our desires to self-knowledge and a purposeful life. For this, I thank them.

The clients who appear in these pages are composites of the actual life stories and individual struggles of people I have seen in psychotherapy so as to disguise the identities of those people. For psychotherapy to be effective it must be confidential. That is a base on which it rests. Consequently, I cannot reveal the identities of those whom I know in this unique way. But the stories you read here are "true" all the same, because the emotional themes and the psychological images emerge directly from the lives of real people.

My second greatest resource in writing this, and all my other books, is my husband and life partner, Ed Epstein. He has argued each major idea with me, critiqued my writing, looked for typos, run the errands, done the photocopying, fixed the dinners, and found me newer and better back supports throughout the creation of this book. He and I have a karmic bond. We were meant to be together doing these things as a team. I could not have done this book without his help.

So many other people have talked with me about the ideas you find here. Demaris Wehr, Amber Rickert, and Heidi Yockey are always intelligent conversationalists whose insights have helped me explore the complexities of female life—and they are also wonderful friends. My research assistant, Katherine Masís, has been an outstanding aid in tracking down scholarly sources and finding the empirical studies to back up my claims. She is the author of most of the endnotes and the careful documenter of many of the materials I have used to illustrate the problems and struggles that characterize female self-determination in our society. I am very thankful to have had these women as colleagues and companions in doing this book.

My editor, Sharon Broll, has been another extraordinary colleague. Perceptive, intelligent, and critical-minded, she is a gifted editor who has a special ability to trim my prose and arrange my ideas into a logical sequence.

My editor at Harmony Books, Shaye Areheart, has been encouraging and enthusiastic about this book from the day I met her. Her energy and belief gave me confidence that there would be an audience for a book that challenges widely held ideas about female power.

My literary agent, Beth Vesel, worked with me for months on the proposal for this book. At first I thought it would be a book "about desire," but Beth disagreed and insisted that I knew more about female desire than I did about desire in general. She was right. Her insight and prodding are always important in the process of planning a book; I am very thankful that Beth and I have been coconspirators for so many years now.

Many of my ideas derive from various teachings of Buddhism, Jung, psychoanalysis, and feminism. Without these important anchors for my life, I would be someone entirely different—perhaps unable to explore the levels and layers of human desire and subjectivity. I only hope that what I have written in these pages will be of use to others in a way that continues and expands the sources in which my ideas are rooted.

Contents

Introduction

IN TWENTY YEARS of practicing psychoanalysis and psychotherapy, I have found that the question What do you want? produces bewilderment in most women. We often do not know or we cannot say what we desire. As a psychoanalyst and a Buddhist, I have learned many theories and explanations of desire, but the problem of female desire—why we are so confused about what we want—always remained. This book is an in-depth look at the problem and a guide to its resolution for women and those who love them.

Human desire has two contrasting faces. The meaner face of desire appears in craving, impulsiveness, addiction, and power mongering. The kinder face shows through self-determination and self-responsibility. We women have learned to hide the meaner face, even from ourselves. Because we often ignore or deny our meaner desires, we are also unfamiliar with how to direct our lives through taking responsibility for our own needs and motives.

Living by our self-determination remains remarkably opaque to us, even in this period when feminism has opened many new opportunities and avenues for female development. If anything we seem blinder than ever to the implications of our own choices and decisions. Whereas in the past we were eager to push the limits of personal sovereignty, we now seem afraid of the freedom that we have. We seek guarantees that our decisions will be approved by others, and that our choices are "right," before we have even understood their implications for ourselves.

In our society the question of desire is often asked with the emphasis on *you*: "What do *you* want?" Over the years of asking it in psychotherapy and psychoanalysis, I have come to change the emphasis: "What do you *want*?" is a question about our intentions. Knowing these, even the unconscious ones, allows us to be responsible for ourselves and our effects on others. In all domains of our lives—appearance, sex, motherhood, career, money, spirituality—we hesitate to break the rules, to move beyond the boundaries that have been set for us over the centuries by male standards and desires. This limits us in becoming aware of our actual desires and in living by our own intentions.

In the pages that follow, I show why breaking the rules and moving beyond the boundaries is necessary for living as self-determining women. We have to awaken to the fact that we were never really meant to be fully enfranchised human beings in patriarchy, so we cannot follow the old rules in becoming fully human.

In Buddhism there is a teaching called the Wheel of Life. It is depicted as a great circle containing six realms of existence.

These realms can be understood as psychological states—states of mind—or as actual places. In Buddhism they are understood to be both. By their simplest names the six are the realms of lowest hell, hungry ghosts, power gods, animals, humans, and gods. Each of these forms exemplifies particular kinds of suffering and certain possibilities for freedom from that suffering. No beings in existence are free from adversity and anguish, but humans have the greatest possibility of liberating themselves. Humans are the only beings who can change their lives through changing their intentions and actions. At the very essence of what it means to be human, then, is the freedom to change. And this can be realized only when we know our own intentions, when we know what we want.

Women and Desire

ONE

Wanting to Be Wanted

A BOUT TEN YEARS AGO, while reading a biography of
the French psychoanalyst Jacques Lacan, I came across
something he said about women that struck me as uncom‑
fortably true: women want to be *wanted*, not to be loved.
He meant that women sought to be desirable rather than to
be fully known. Lacan arrived at this conclusion after years
of psychoanalyzing and seducing women. (That is to say, he
attempted to psychoanalyze some women and to seduce others.
A heavily rationalized womanizer, he seduced many women,
but I doubt that he successfully psychoanalyzed any.) A some‑
times brilliant theoretician, Lacan was also sexist and terribly
arrogant, so I wondered if I could take his claim seriously. Yet,
despite my doubt, the idea stayed with me.

Over the ensuing years I read many feminist accounts
of female desire, but I came across nothing quite as bold and

blatant as Lacan's claim. A psychoanalyst myself, I am also a feminist, a mother and a wife, a writer, a teacher of psychotherapy, and a student of Buddhism. In all of these roles I find it useful to keep my ears and eyes open to the unspoken, the unwritten, and the unconscious. So while I tucked away the idea of women wanting to be wanted and continued to go about my business of seeing people in individual psychotherapy, Jungian analysis, and couples therapy, in the back of my mind this notion was having an effect. That women might be driven by the desire to be desirable, rather than by the desire to be known and loved, became the background music for much that I heard about female desire both in and out of psychotherapy for the next ten years.

I now believe that Lacan was basically right about the problem of female desire, but instead of seeing it as a normal aspect of female character, as he believed, I see it as a damaging *affliction* of female development in societies where women are expected to please men. The compulsion to be desired and desirable undermines self-direction, self-confidence, and self-determination in women from adolescence through old age, in all our roles, from daughter to mother, from lover to wife, from student to worker or leader, whether or not the affliction is conscious.

Wanting to be wanted is about finding our power in an image rather than in our own actions. We try to appear attractive, nice, good, valid, legitimate, or worthy to someone else, instead of discovering what we actually feel and want for ourselves. In this kind of conscious or unconscious arrangement, other people are expected to provide our own feelings of power, worth, or vitality, at the expense of our authentic development. We then feel resentful, frustrated, and out of control because we have sacrificed our real needs and desires to the arrangements we have made with others. We find ourselves always wanting to be seen in a positive light: the perfect mother, the ideal friend, the seductive lover, the slender or athletic body, the kind neighbor, the competent boss. In place of knowing the truth of who we are and what we want from our lives, we become trapped in images.

Wanting to be wanted is not codependency. It's not something that develops out of someone else's needs or demands. Rather, it is a desire for power and control that has been transformed and hidden. Instead of learning how to fulfill this—our own—desire, we learn gradually, but clearly, how to fulfill others'. This dynamic is rooted in the widespread psychological and social constraints on female power. For, in spite of feminism, female power—decisiveness, status, command, influence—cannot be expressed directly at home or in the workplace without arousing suspicion, confusion, fear, or dread. Both women and men still tend to experience female power as exotic at best and dangerous and despicable at worst. Lacking clear avenues for developing our power directly, we learn to be indirect in making emotional arrangements based on others' needs and wants, and how we would like to be seen.

Nor is wanting to be wanted the expression of a desire for intimacy or closeness. Rather, wanting to be wanted makes us feel as though we have no clear desires of our own. We focus on how to bring things under control by appearing in a certain way, speaking in a certain manner, implying our needs. Yet we never say directly what we want, and we may never actually know. We have been culturally programmed so thoroughly to tune in to the subtleties of whether or not we are having the "desired effect" that we fail to tune in to what we really want or to see how strongly we are motivated by wanting to be wanted.

Many times in individual and couples psychotherapy, I have faced a woman and said, "What do you want here?" and she has replied, "I really don't know" or "This is what the children and my husband need" or "What do *you* think?" If I push further and gently ask her to come up with some answer—any answer—she usually gets flustered and apologetic. She either doesn't know or is afraid to say what she wants.

Female Power

IN 1987 PSYCHOLOGIST Florence Wiedemann and I published a book titled *Female Authority: Empowering Women Through Psychotherapy,* in which we detailed a condition that we called the double bind of female authority: women are damned if they claim their authority (they are called controlling, dominating, bitches, or even feminazis) and damned if they don't (they are called manipulative, dependent, depressed, or worse, immature and self-defeating). We addressed the problem that results when girls and women believe that authority and knowledge lie wholly outside themselves—in men, gods, or institutions such as school or church. Since then I have helped many women in psychotherapeutic and educational settings to restore their personal authority, claim their competence and voices, and seek satisfaction in their lives.

Yet as successful as many of these women have become, they often feel "out of control" in their personal lives. Although they can speak openly and passionately about the values and principles they believe in, and defend others' rights, they still resist claiming and asserting personal needs and desires, especially when these are in conflict with others'. They fear being seen as too bossy or too self-absorbed.

Anne is just such a woman, in her midforties, whom I have come to know through weekly sessions of psychotherapy over the past two years. She is a professor and part-time dean at a local college. Articulate, conscientious, always prepared for her therapy meetings, Anne appears to others to be in control of her life. She is the mother of three lively children, one son and two daughters, the eldest of whom is away at college. Her children do well academically and socially. She is married to a "nice guy"—a laid-back professional who spends a lot of his free time outdoors with their children, camping, hiking, skiing. He's also an egalitarian spouse who runs the kitchen and chauffeurs the kids. Anne appreciates all of this about John, especially his parenting skills.

A grateful feminist, Anne enjoys both her career and her family. She is decisive, well regarded as a leader at work, and admired by her many friends. Certainly no one would dub her a crybaby or victim. On the surface Anne appears to have every reason to be completely happy and satisfied with her life.

You may know someone like Anne who seems to have it all; you may even envy her. But each week when I meet with Anne, she is full of complaints. She talks mostly about feeling that her life is out of her control: she never has a moment to herself, is almost always overwhelmed and overworked. She has no time for her own creative outlet, a combination of sculpting and painting, and she feels dominated by others' needs and demands. The disparity between how Anne appears and what she feels about herself and her life is a symptom of wanting to be wanted.

Anne's compulsion to be desirable begins with the fundamental belief that power—the right, capacity, or authority to act or influence others on her behalf—is not legitimately hers but resides in the eye of the beholder. She struggles mightily with how she is seen by others, not wanting anyone to think she is demanding or pushy. Anne often tells me about feeling empty—lost, betrayed, or abandoned. Sometimes in a dream she is alone in a large building or tent and does not know which way to turn or if there is anyone who can help.

Anne resents many of the things she has agreed to do at work and at home, even with her friends. She recently spent the evening with a good friend who took hours to recount the details of a trek she and her partner had taken through some mountains in South America. Anne felt she had no choice but to listen because the friend had invited Anne for dinner specifically to tell her about the trip. Anne appeared to listen agreeably, although she was bored and even angry. I asked her why she had accepted the invitation in the first place if she didn't want to spend the evening hearing about the trip. "I don't know," she replied. "I couldn't imagine turning it down. After all, this friend has spent a lot of time listening to me bitch and moan about my job."

"And so you set aside your own desire to spend the evening quietly at home?" I inquired.

"Actually, no," Anne said. "You see, I didn't know how resentful I really felt until I was sitting there, feeling under her control with no chance of going home. Of course, I couldn't tell her how I felt. I would never say something that sounds so rejecting to a friend. I wouldn't want to hurt her feelings."

To her friend it appeared that Anne chose to spend the evening together, but Anne had actually felt coerced by her own compulsion to be desirable. In order to make a choice, Anne had to have at least two options. Being free to *choose* means having alternatives, and in this case Anne would have needed to feel that she could say no in order to give a truthful yes. No one but Anne can make such a personal choice, but she has unknowingly refused to make it and so feels herself to be under the power of another.

Anne's compulsion to appear agreeable unintentionally leads her to deceive her friend. Like most of us Anne wants to appear supportive of others and their needs, but she does not take full responsibility even for this desire. If Anne really *wanted* to appear supportive, then her decision to go to her friend's would be freely given. But because Anne's compulsion to be desirable is hidden from her, she feels robbed of her power and control in the presence of her friend. The hidden compulsion to be wanted puts us under a sort of magic spell that makes our behavior confusing to others, even to ourselves. We seem to have *chosen* to be in a situation—a dinner party, a committee meeting, even a marriage—but we feel as though we had no choice, so we are there resentfully, holding in our negative emotions with arms crossed and a plastered smile sealing our lips.

What Do Women Really Want?

THE QUESTION What do women really want? is often attributed to Sigmund Freud, but as far as I know its first formal appearance is in a medieval folktale titled "The Marriage of Sir Gawain and the Lady Ragnell," whose earliest recorded version is from the thirteenth century. Its origin likely goes back further than this version because elements of its plot and themes show up in other folktales and literature in England (such as "The Wife of Bath's Tale" from Chaucer's *Canterbury*

Tales) and throughout Europe, indicating that it was widely known by the thirteenth or fourteenth century. Since then it has been told and retold in many forms throughout the world.

The following rendition most closely resembles a modern retelling published in *The Maid of the North: Feminist Folk Tales from Around the World*, edited by Ethel Johnston Phelps. Phelps selected stories in which the female characters, especially the heroines, contrast with those of the traditional fairy tales and folktales that are commonly told to us as children. On the one hand, the heroines of our most popular children's tales, like *Cinderella* and *Sleeping Beauty*, are known mostly for their beauty, grace, or generosity—and their submissiveness to Prince Charming. The tales chosen by Phelps, on the other hand, portray women as strong, capable, and resourceful, as well as hardworking and self-determining.

GAWAIN AND THE LADY RAGNELL

One day, King Arthur was out hunting a great white stag at the edge of the oak woods when he looked up and found himself confronted by a tall, powerful chieftain, swinging his sword and appearing as if he would cut down the king on the spot. This man was Sir Gromer, who declared that he was seeking revenge for the loss of some of his northern lands to Arthur. Since Arthur was unarmed, Sir Gromer showed the king mercy and gave him a chance to save his life.

Gromer issued a challenge: the king had one year to return unarmed to this spot with an answer to the question What do women desire above all else? If Arthur answered the question correctly, his life would be spared; if not, he would lose his head.

Arthur agreed, but he was very discouraged. This must be a trick question, he thought. He felt certain that no one knew the answer. Back at the castle Arthur told the entire story to his nephew Sir Gawain, who was known as the wisest, bravest, most compassionate and courteous of all the Knights of the Round Table. The young knight, in contrast to the king, was hopeful. He and Arthur had a year to search the kingdom, and he was certain they would find the right answer.

Almost a year passed, and Arthur and Gawain collected many answers, but not one had the ring of truth. The appointed day was almost upon them when one morning Arthur rode out alone through the purple heather and golden gorse, deep in thought about his predicament. At the edge of the oak woods, he was suddenly confronted by a large, grotesque woman who was covered with warts and almost as wide as she was tall.

Her eyes met his fearlessly as she declared, "You are Arthur, the king, and in two days you must meet Sir Gromer with an answer to a question."

"Yes," Arthur replied hesitantly, "but how do you know about this?"

"I am the Lady Ragnell, and Sir Gromer is my stepbrother. You don't have the right answer, do you?"

"I have many answers, and I don't see how it concerns you," Arthur retorted, gathering his reins to turn and ride home.

"You do not have the right answer," said Ragnell with a confidence that filled Arthur with gloom. "I have the answer."

Arthur turned and leaped off his horse. "Tell me the answer and I will give you a large bag of gold!"

"I have no use for gold," Ragnell replied calmly.

"Nonsense, woman, you can buy anything you want with it! What do you want, then? Jewelry, land? Whatever you want, I will pay you—that is, if you have the right answer."

"I know the answer. I can promise you that," responded Ragnell. After a slight pause she added, "I demand in return that Sir Gawain become my husband."

Arthur gasped. "Impossible!" he shouted. "You ask the impossible, woman. I cannot give you my nephew. He's his own man, not mine to give!"

"I did not ask you to *give* me the knight Gawain. If Gawain agrees to marry me of his own free will, then I will give you the answer. Those are my terms."

"Terms! What right do you have to give *me* terms? It's impossible! I could never bring him such a proposal."

Ragnell stared calmly at the king's face and simply said, "If you should change your mind, I will be here tomorrow." Then she disappeared into the woods.

Shaken from this strange encounter, Arthur rode home at a slow pace, thinking to himself that he could never speak to Gawain of this matter. The loathsome woman! How dare she ask for the finest knight in marriage! But the afternoon air was soft, and the fateful meeting with Gromer weighed heavily on Arthur. When the king returned to the castle, he found himself telling his nephew about his adventure, concluding, "She knows the answer, I'm sure of it—but I didn't intend to tell you any of this."

Gawain smiled sweetly, not yet knowing Ragnell's specific proposal. "But this is good news, Uncle. Why do you sound so discouraged?"

With his eyes averted, the king reported Ragnell's demand, along with a detailed description of her grotesque face, warty skin, and bulging size.

"How fortunate that I can save your life!" replied Gawain immediately. Over his uncle's protests Gawain stated, "It is my choice and my decision. I will return with you tomorrow and agree to the marriage, on the condition that her answer saves your life."

Early the next morning Gawain rode out with Arthur to meet the Lady Ragnell. Even seeing her face-to-face did not shake Gawain's resolve. Her proposal was accepted, and Gawain bowed to her courteously. "If tomorrow your answer saves the king's life, we shall be wed."

On the fateful morning Gawain rode out part of the way with Arthur, who assured the knight that he would try all the other answers first.

The tall, powerful chieftain was waiting for Arthur, his broadsword gleaming in the sun. As Arthur read out one answer after another, Gromer shouted, "No! No! No!" until at last he raised his sword high above his head. "Wait!" the king cried. "I have one more answer. What a woman desires above all else is the power of sovereignty, the right to exercise her own free will."

With a loud oath Gromer dropped his sword to his side. "You didn't find that answer on your own! My cursed stepsister Ragnell gave it to you! I'll cut off her head. I'll run her through with my sword!" He turned and plunged back into the forest, a string of curses echoing after him.

Arthur returned to where Gawain waited with the Lady Ragnell. All three rode back to the castle in silence. Only Ragnell seemed in good spirits.

The news spread quickly through the castle that a bizarre wedding was to take place between an ugly hag and the magnificent Gawain. No one could imagine what had per-suaded Gawain to marry this creature. Some thought she must possess great lands and estates. Others thought she must have some secret magic. Most were just stunned at the fate of poor Gawain.

King Arthur drew his nephew aside. "A postponement might be in order," he said.

"I gave her my promise, Uncle. Would you have me break my word?" Gawain replied.

So the wedding took place in the abbey, and the strange wedding feast was held before the entire court. Throughout the long day and evening, Gawain remained pleasant and courteous. In no way did he show anything but kind attention to his bride.

At last the wedding couple retired to their chamber. "You have kept your promise well and faithfully," Ragnell observed. "You've shown me neither pity nor revulsion. Come kiss me now that we are wedded."

Gawain went to her at once and kissed her. When he stepped aside before him stood a serene, beautiful woman with gray eyes and a smiling face. His scalp tingled with shock, and he jumped back. "What manner of sorcery is this?"

Ragnell replied, "Do you prefer me in this form?" as she turned slowly in a full circle.

"Yes, of course, but I don't understand," stammered Gawain, confused and frightened.

"My stepbrother Gromer has always hated me. He obtained a knowledge of sorcery from his mother and used it to change me into a monstrous hag. He commanded me to live in that shape until the finest knight in Britain willingly chose me as his bride."

"But why did he hate you so cruelly?" asked Gawain.

With her lips curled in amusement, Ragnell stated, "He thought me bold and unwomanly because I refused his commands, for both my property and my person."

With great admiration Gawain said, "Then you have won the impossible condition, and his evil spell is broken!"

"Only in part, my dear Gawain." Her eyes held his steadily. "You have a choice which way I will be. Would you have me in this, my own shape, at night in our chamber? Or would you have me grotesque in our chamber at night and my own shape by day in the castle? Fair by night, or fair by day—think carefully before you choose."

Gawain knelt before his bride and responded at once. "It is a choice I cannot make. It concerns you, my dear Ragnell, and only you can choose. Whatever you choose, I will willingly abide by it."

Ragnell released a long, deep breath. The radiance in her face overwhelmed him.

"You have answered well, dearest Gawain. Your answer has broken Gromer's evil spell completely. The last condition he set was that, after the marriage, the greatest knight in Britain, my husband, must give me the power of sovereignty, the right to exercise my own free will. Only then would the wicked enchantment be broken forever."

And so in wonder and joy began the marriage of Sir Gawain and the Lady Ragnell.

Hag Psychology and the Mythical Dangers of Female Desire

THIS ANCIENT STORY holds dimensions of meaning that are much deeper than its entertaining surface. It is a tale not only about self-determination and self-confidence in women but also about the confinement of a traditional patriarchal marriage, which, when the story was set down in written text, required by law that a woman surrender her freedom and property to her husband. Indeed, I am certain that this folktale was told as a warning to women and men about the psychological and interpersonal dangers of a condition that eliminated a woman's personal sovereignty.

In the medieval period, when the tale originated, the power of the mythical hag to rob people of their vitality was well-known to audiences. The hag was said to ride the bodies of men and children at night while they were sleeping, absorbing their vigor into herself. In the morning her victims would wake to feeble will and lifeless gloom. Her kiss was her most potent weapon. Getting close to her lips meant risking having your soul sucked out. A medieval audience would have appreciated Gawain's courage in kissing his bride so directly. They would also have guessed that he performed this act without hesitation because he sensed Ragnell's true nature. He would have been thought to have seen beyond her appearance in order to trust that she was not really a destructive hag who would exhaust and dominate him.

Stories about the evil power of the hag were one way that earlier societies demeaned and demonized female power. Portraying female power as devitalizing, overwhelming, poisonous—especially for unsuspecting men and children—encouraged a belief in a negative emotional spell that could be cast exclusively by a demanding woman.

Today when women want to be wanted they unintentionally reinforce the misogynist belief that a demanding woman is to be dreaded and subdued. When we act as though our desires are too powerful and can overtake another's free will or good sense, we reinvent the negative psychology of the hag-bitch. We are at risk of identifying ourselves and our desires with an alien, almost superhuman emotional power.

When Anne, for example, prefaces her own needs or wants with phrases such as "Do you mind if I . . ." or "It would be so nice if you . . . ," she implies that she wants something especially burdensome or difficult that cannot be stated directly. When we cloak our desires in niceties and seductions, we protect ourselves from being known directly and imply that others must always be nice to us. This kind of eggshell quality of female desire suggests that our needs must be hidden, that they are dangerous.

In therapy sessions I often remind people that direct requests for reassurance, appreciation, even compliments are necessary when the need is urgent. Women frequently challenge me, saying, "That spoils the effect. People should just give these things spontaneously." My response is that there are no shoulds when it comes to such interpersonal supports, and that clear and direct communication avoids the indirect message that others must intuit our desires. Attempting to evoke responses from others without claiming one's needs not only is confusing but carries the hidden meaning of danger—that something is so troubling it cannot be put into words.

It is only when we speak directly, with a secure self-confidence, that we step outside this negative meaning of female desire. Recognizing our desires as human-size (rather than monstrous) means that we can speak about them calmly and clearly. Although she was doomed to be a loathsome lady, Ragnell knew that her needs and desires were acceptable. She made her demands to King Arthur in a way that showed confidence in herself and her knowledge that Gawain had a choice in responding to her. She did not apologize, nor did she blame. She spoke boldly from her heart.

But, as many women have pointed out to me, Ragnell does not win her freedom all by herself. She has to conform to the conditions set by her stepbrother: that the greatest knight in all of Britain must agree to marry her, and that this knight, her husband, must grant her the power of her own sovereignty, the right to make her own choices. For some readers these conditions seem to diminish Ragnell's accomplishments. But we should not be too literal in our understanding of this tale.

The story of Ragnell symbolizes the development of a woman's self-determination within the confines of a patriarchal tradition that demanded that she give up her rights and property after she married. Ragnell has to depend on men in power to assist her in becoming a free agent, but that is not so different from our situation today. At no point is Ragnell passive, compliant, or indirect. She defies her stepbrother and finds a way to meet his conditions. She even confronts the king, telling him that he does not know what a woman desires. She watches her new husband carefully, and she skillfully presents her challenge to be taken seriously (to kiss her) at a moment when it is likely to be most effective. And, ultimately, she is aware that she cannot become self-determining without relying on others; she poses her questions to Gawain to test him, to see if he has grasped the fundamental dilemma of her life.

Ragnell symbolizes a process through which a woman claims the authority to be her own person, to command her own actions. When we first meet her, she is the dreaded hag-bitch, the symbol of the emotionally demanding woman. Yet we can tell that she is something more, for even the king is convinced of her wisdom. As the story progresses we are won over by her courage and good humor. We are pleased that she will not be humiliated or subdued by the opinions of others. And finally, when Gawain comes forward to kiss her, we believe that he also senses something different about her. Of course he *is* startled by her transformation, as are we. What of this transformation? Not until Gawain kneels before her and answers well do we fully understand that she has been transformed not by his kiss but by the process of her own courage in pursuing her freedom and confronting her new husband.

By example, Ragnell shows us how to respond to the constraints of patriarchy in order to become a self-determining woman. First, she keeps her own counsel in the face of challenge. Although by all standards she is ugly, she is unconcerned about her appearance and definite in her stance. She is who she is. She speaks from her own authority in challenging her stepbrother and the king. She feels free to arrange her life according to her desires, even though she may be at risk for retaliations. She is knowledgeable about her desire for personal sovereignty, and she will not be discouraged by spells cast on her, insults, or rejections. She will not have her motives demeaned, even by the king.

The False Power of the Muse

To understand why, many hundreds of years later, it is still such a struggle for women to follow Ragnell's lead, we need to look more closely at the curse of her stepbrother, Gromer, who thought Ragnell was too bold and unwomanly in refusing his commands. She was a threat to his male dominance, the prototype of the uppity woman. So her stepbrother turned her into his image of that threat—an ugly, frightening hag, an emasculating bitch. His wish was that Ragnell would stay that way forever, but her self-determination was more than Gromer had bargained for. She stepped outside his spell in commanding her own life.

This move to shame female desire by turning it into the image of a hag-bitch is matched by a countermove to elevate female beauty and grace into positions of purported power. If female desire is stifled through male dominance, how can women be attracted to fill their designated roles as wife or mother, as worker or lover? They are promised other means for attaining power, means that remain under male control. *Female power is beauty* is the refrain that influences young women everywhere to believe that they will have influence and status if they employ the "right" images.

Throughout the centuries of patriarchal art and literature, we find a recurring image of the desire-awakening maiden (to be discussed in greater detail in the next chapter), who is portrayed as the exact opposite of the devitalizing hag. This muse is the essence of vitality and life, whereas the hag is the essence of suffocation and death.

Today's muse appears in the form of an anorectic woman-child. Her image is girlish or waiflike, with a blank stare. It's hard to imagine that she is meant to be enlivening and arousing, but there is no doubt that she is the blueprint for fashion and female beauty in the contemporary world, emulated by young women everywhere. Her principal roles in our culture are supermodel, ingenue, celebrity, and movie star. Whatever her form at any cultural moment, though, the muse stirs fascination, inspiration, and procreation in her male admirers and, by extension, in all of us.

But the muse is not her own person. She is always under the control of her master: he is the Subject and she is the Object of Desire. A woman who identifies with being the Object of

Desire is not a source of her own inspiration; she does not feel as though her life belongs to her. Her vitality and imagination, her efforts and plans, are directed toward the desires of others, toward being desirable as the anorectic woman-child, the lovely lady, the self-sacrificing mother. To be the Object of Desire means to have no core self, no clear autonomy and self-determination that are under your command. Ragnell, even in her beautiful form, is no muse because she is the Subject of her own desires.

By contrast, being the Subject of your own desires does not preclude having an attractive appearance or a pleasant manner. But appearance, manner, niceness, self-sacrifice are never the central motivators for the woman who is a Subject. She—like Ragnell—speaks confidently and clearly even in the face of challenge, conflict, and her own anxiety. Because she wants to be known for who she is, instead of how she appears, she is straightforward and direct.

Why, then, in spite of the recent waves of feminism, do we continue to worship the muse? Because we continue to believe that female power is unhealthy and overwhelming—a kind of soul-sucking danger that needs to be warded off by women and men alike. So we unconsciously support the male fantasy that the only *legitimate* power to be encouraged in girls and women is to be the Object of Desire.

Women and men alike dread the hag-bitch. Women do not want to be identified as too demanding, pushy, bossy. We do not want to be known as the type who intimidates others with ultimatums, demands, or needs that might overwhelm. In our rush away from the hag-bitch, we move toward the muse and her false power as the Object of Desire. Although she appears to promise that female power *is* beauty, she denies a woman the right to her own sovereignty. The muse always remains under the control of the master; it is the master's life that is enhanced and completed through her inspiration.

Nowhere can we see this more clearly than in Diana, Princess of Wales, the cultural muse of our time. Diana is the embodiment of a collective Object of Desire, a muse for the contemporary world. We used her image to inspire and excite us. Our hunger for her vitalizing effects is the crucial aspect of Diana's public appeal, in both her life and her death.

Diana herself was tragically caught in the female-power-is-beauty belief. Witness her much-maligned fate: to be pursued relentlessly by publicists, photographers, and a public who felt that she belonged to them, and whom she courted tirelessly in her quest for stardom. Diana obsessively maintained a slender appearance, leading at one point to an eating disorder in which she vomited up to four times a day. Even after she had overcome this dangerous condition, she carefully controlled her diet and exercise. She was fatefully, desperately motivated by wanting to be wanted.

The ultimate Object of Desire, Diana sought romantic relationships with untrustworthy partners, starting with the Prince of Wales. She may have been loved to some degree by each of her suitors, but their motives were mixed at best. Most of all they wanted her for what she symbolized rather than for the person she was. They used the power of her appearance, and her difficulties with self-esteem, to their own advantage and status. They did not return that power to her, as Gawain did to Ragnell. Diana was cursed as a muse as Ragnell was cursed as a hag. And, as we will see, the curse of the muse is often the more devastating: although the hag may not be wanted, or even loved, she can know her own desires if she chooses. The muse cannot, for as soon as she does, she ceases to be the muse.

Diana is a symbol of female desire at the end of the twentieth century. She portrays the conflict and confusion, shame and fascination of potentially liberated women trying to be Objects of Desire. We haunted her with our need to live vicariously through her, to be enlivened by her, until the tragic accident of her death expressed how brutally high the stakes are in this game. Tragically, Diana will always remain an Object of Desire—tragically because at the time of her death she was beginning to move toward the goal of claiming her own desires.

A Matter of Heart

DURING AND AFTER her divorce, Diana spoke out truthfully and became a role model for other women who, in hearing about her personal struggles, seemed to feel a promise of release from their own shame and family secrets. As psychologist Carol Gilligan remarked, "In breaking out so publicly from an imprisonment of silence enforced by shame, Diana discovered that in speaking from her heart, she touched the hearts of others. Rather than shunning her, people embraced her. Because she felt psychologically homeless and shunned, she could reach out without the shadow of condescension to those who were physically homeless and to people shunned because of AIDS and leprosy." Admitting her vulnerabilities while maintaining her image of the desire-awakening maiden, Diana cracked open the belief that beauty alone can protect even a fairy-tale princess. Yet because of her untimely death, Diana may be remembered more for her beauty—that "effervescent, bubbly intoxication," as one reporter put it—than for her final courageous refusal to hide in shame and silence, unless we change our understanding of female desire.

Speaking the truth, as Diana had begun to do, is the only path out of the superficiality and false promises of wanting to be wanted to the possibilities of being loved. If wanting to be wanted is a matter of *image*, then wanting to be loved is a matter of *heart*. Being loved is being known in our own fallible, open, true spirit. As Ragnell shows us, being true to yourself does not mean judging or blaming or letting your tongue roll with nasty, accusatory words. Rather, it means speaking your own thoughts and feelings with respect for others, without trying to cover up the harsh bits or the rough edges in order to keep your image shiny and clean.

When we live by the truth, we discover what constitutes not only our individual nature but also our fundamental humanity. Yet speaking the truth can expose us to criticism and judgment, and most of all to our own fears about the nature of our desires. Admitting who we are and what we want, recognizing our dependence and gratitude, puts us in a vulnerable position. We learn that human strengths and abilities are always limited by weakness, tiredness, forgetfulness, bad habits, and other imperfections. These innate limitations awaken us to the ways we need others and compel us to appreciate how we are helped and sustained by our relationships. Hiding from the truth leads only to the opposite: anxious self-protectiveness, isolation, fear, and shame.

Hiding in the Woods

ALL OF US STRUGGLE with shame, hiding ourselves and our needs because they seem to be wrong or bad. Diana's eating disorder was at its worst during the time she felt shamed by the rejection of her husband in favor of his mistress. Unconsciously she attempted to control those feelings by obsessively controlling her body, appearing to be slender while consuming huge amounts of food. She hid from herself and the world the ways in which she felt empty and hungry, wanting to be filled by someone else's desire.

The woods where the Lady Ragnell lived as a hag can be understood as a *symbol* of shame—a place where we hide when we feel our identity or desires are bad. Although Ragnell does not express the feeling of shame, we can imagine that she lived a lonely, isolated life as the hag in the woods, awaiting a time when she could step forward. Women who identify with being the hag-bitch—the negatively powerful woman—almost always hide because they feel ashamed.

Shame is an emotion that expresses the desire to hide, disappear, or even die because we fear that the self is empty, bad, or inferior. When we are ashamed it feels as though nothing can be done about it, because shame is linked to a sense of *being*, not something that we're doing. If you believe you cannot do anything about feeling that there is something wrong with who you are, then it makes sense that you would try to protect yourself from being exposed. When we feel ashamed all kinds of deceits and lies arise in us to provide a protective cover.

When I think of Ragnell's woods as a symbol of shame, I think of women hiding in unsatisfactory, sometimes uncommitted, even cruel and abusive relationships. In such a shame-based environment, women are intimidated by name-calling, betrayal, threats of violence, and actual violence, which are often interpreted as indicating that something is terribly wrong with the women themselves. I also think of the more ordinary problem of a man who says to his female partner, "I just need more space, some time away from you so that I can get my thoughts together." This kind of statement implies that the woman sucks up the space between them, filling it with her overwhelming presence. In this example the image of the soul-sucking hag creeps into what many regard as an egalitarian dialogue between the sexes—rationalized by pop psychology about a man's need to separate himself from a woman in order to possess himself, as though the woman's presence prevents that experience.

When Cheryl began psychotherapy with me, she was thirty-three years old, single, very intelligent, well-educated, and working as a partner in a mostly male law firm in Philadelphia. Of medium height, she weighed about 145 pounds and felt very ashamed of her weight and her body. Although she was muscular and healthy, she constantly felt that something was wrong with the way she looked. Cheryl was romantically involved with Brad, who was twenty-five, good-looking, energetic, less educated, and extremely noncommittal. They had been involved for about a year, and things were not going well. But Cheryl didn't want to talk about their relationship. She wanted to talk about herself, because she was afraid something was really wrong with her. As had Princess Diana, Cheryl was choosing men who eventually betrayed her, sexually or financially. Before Brad she had fallen for two other men who quickly professed love for her, promptly moved into her apartment, and soon began to take advantage of her high income and low self-esteem.

Cheryl wanted to get married and start a family but had no idea how to go about it. She did not want to "pressure" Brad, who was still finishing college. In fact, she did not even want to speak about her desires to Brad, because she feared bringing up marriage and family would scare him away. Cheryl said she just wanted to appear to be "hanging out" with Brad in a relaxed and open way so that he could see that she wasn't the type of woman to pressure him.

After Cheryl had been in therapy with me for about two years, living off and on with Brad, she finally confronted him: she was no longer willing to wait for him to make up his mind. She wanted him to commit to a long-term relationship, with marriage in tow, or she would move on. In spite of her forceful declaration, however, Cheryl was not fully convinced of her worth and attractiveness. Undermined by feelings of shame about her body and afraid that no man would choose her, Cheryl blurted out complaints and blame. She said she was "disgusted" that Brad had stayed with her for so many years without making any promises about their future. Instead of speaking responsibly, she blamed Brad for making her feel so bad about herself. Her feelings of shame had kept her in the woods too long.

Unconsciously Cheryl acted out Brad's worst image of the hag-bitch: the power-hungry monster who cannot be satisfied. This fantasy of the dangerous hag depends on the belief that her demands and desires are endless, voracious, consuming. When women identify with shame, they believe that they are empty or worthless and turn to others to fill them up with supports and reassurances. As long as shame is primary in a woman's identity, nothing will fill the void; shame is like a vacuum or black hole that cannot hold the compliments and reassurances that are offered.

Cheryl gave Brad two weeks to make up his mind, but Brad turned her down after two days. Naturally, Cheryl was angry, bereft, and somewhat inclined to blame me and her therapy for compelling her to speak directly and "spoil" her relationship. Gradually, Cheryl and I examined the beliefs and fantasies that linked her to the feeling of shame. We discovered why she had been attracted to so many elusive and irresponsible men over the years and why she still longed to be shown that she was not a bitchy woman who spoiled a man's space or destroyed his soul.

As we went through this process, Cheryl learned more about her psychological complexes, the name Carl Jung gave to the emotional tendencies we all have to protect ourselves in the same ways we did in childhood, to imagine a world that is filled with the dangers we sensed and encountered in our original families. These complexes are unconscious and semi-conscious tendencies to act out emotional dramas that may or may not be known to us, fueled by habits acquired in our dependency bonds from infancy and childhood, with parents and siblings.

When Cheryl faced Brad directly with her desires, she feared he would say she was not physically attractive to him. She also feared he would blame her for being unfair to him, for wanting too much, despite the fact that she had been endlessly fair and generous. This made sense only when we discovered that Cheryl had been both attracted to and intimidated by her unpredictable father when she was a child. A charming Bad Boy, her father was also a prominent lawyer who was outwardly respected by the community. He was a "street angel" and a "house devil," as Cheryl put it. A womanizer, Cheryl's father humiliated his wife and blamed her for his failure to feel love for her after the first years of their marriage.

Cheryl witnessed many fights between her parents but felt more critical of her mother's passivity than of her father's accusations. Cheryl wanted her mother to stand up to her father and claim her own worth. Cheryl determined that *she* would win her father's love and praise by emulating him. She sought his approval by excelling at school in the subjects he loved and by developing a social charm that matched his. She won his admiration and interest to such an extent that eventually she felt as though her father's responses to her, his love and praise, were under *her* control. If he failed to notice her or remark on an accomplishment, she would believe that she must be at fault. Her "power" over him was that of the Object of Desire; she imagined that she controlled him through her actions, image, and accomplishments. This was the father complex that Cheryl re-created with Brad and her other lovers: unconsciously she wanted to be the exclusive Object of Desire, the longed-for companion who would perfectly meet the needs of the man.

Her energies would first be directed to making the man feel good about himself and at home in her life. Then she would seek to be approved and admired for her intelligence and attractiveness. Because she felt ashamed of her body, Cheryl believed that she had to work extra hard at being accommodating and pleasing, so that her partner would remain physically attracted to her. When her partner's interest seemed to wane, Cheryl would try to do something special—to make a particularly good meal or give a nice gift—in order to keep him involved.

Psychological complexes compel us, as they compelled Cheryl, to repeat the emotional themes from childhood, especially in our adult partnerships and parenting. Unless we become conscious of these complexes, they rule us through subjective impulses and images that seem to be reality. Complexes are the psychological karma that we bring with us from our families of origin. We came by them honestly, when we were dependent on others for survival and sustenance. They are triggered in our adult lives not only by certain emotional meanings but also by any stimuli—sounds, tastes, touch, smells, physical states (such as nausea)—familiar from the original contexts that endangered or overstimulated us.

When our complexes are hidden from our awareness, they can become monstrous, dampening our vitality and motivation. The experience of pervasive discontent and a futile kind of inner emptiness are symptoms of hidden complexes in their uglier forms. Unacknowledged longings and fears manifest themselves as strong drives that may appear in dreams and fantasies as demons, snakes, floods, earthquakes, threatening intruders, or hungry ghosts who could consume us. They may appear in waking life as addictions and compulsions that make no logical sense. Indeed, one way to interpret the monstrous hag hiding in the woods is as women's unconscious complex of female power that can be civilized and refined only when it is listened to, examined, and brought out into the light of day.

So Cheryl discovered what had bound her to irresponsible men: she was attracted to men like her father, whom she then idealized and tried to please, failing to notice where they were limited, wrong, or even bad. She would take all the responsibility for what went wrong in the relationships and increase her shame, believing that something was fundamentally wrong with *her* while overlooking the failures and mistakes of her partners.

Today, some five years later, Cheryl is married to a man very different from Daddy. He is a successful lawyer, like Cheryl and her father, but he and Cheryl have a relationship of mutual involvement and friendship. Together they work as professional mediators in divorce and separation cases. Cheryl now teaches other women and men to speak the truth in the context of respect and fairness.

Cheryl's loss of Brad opened the way for a new development. She learned the lesson that Ragnell hints at when she says to Arthur, "I did not ask you to *give* me the knight Gawain. If Gawain agrees to marry me of his own free will . . ." This is the lesson of knowing the boundaries and limitations of your desire and power. When you learn to speak the truth, you come to recognize that you have no special power over others to make them do your bidding. You cannot pressure or scare away others by speaking your desires. Other adults also have free will. We all have a responsibility to speak our own desires and to respect those of others. When you speak the truth directly, you come to know the possibilities and limitations of being the Subject of Desire. For women this means overcoming our fears of being seen as the hag-bitch in order to say clearly and fully what we want without either demanding that we get it or believing that we have taken control of another.

The Subject of Desire

EITHER BECAUSE OF ignorance of the actual meaning of self-determination or because of the magic spell cast by wanting to be wanted, we women often misunderstand or forget that our deepest desire is for sovereignty over our own lives, the right and responsibility to act with free will—to be the Subjects of our own desires. This is true of all human beings, no matter their condition. It is only within the framework of such personal sovereignty that the kinder face of desire can shine and develop, through the responsibility and self-determination to live in a compassionate, conscious manner.

Being the Subject of your desires means not just asserting what you want but taking responsibility for your desires as well. These are closely related but different issues. Whereas being assertive means clearly stating your own needs and desires, taking responsibility carries the additional meaning of answering for yourself, choosing ethically, and being trustworthy. Taking responsibility is the step that follows being assertive. For instance, in therapy clients sometimes say something like "I spoke to my partner about my need for greater reassurance and closeness, and he said, 'Okay. So what am I supposed to do about that?' I was just furious. Obviously he doesn't care at all how I feel."

"So what did you say after he said that?" I ask calmly. The most frequent answer is "Nothing. The conversation was over because he just doesn't get it. I have nothing more to say." The speaker has put the responsibility on the listener to take the conversation forward, but the speaker is the person with the desire. To responsibly handle such a problem, the speaker should continue to communicate her desire.

Being responsible means trying again and again in different ways to say what you want, until it can be heard and understood. If you are trapped in a psychological complex, in feeling that (for example) you are *never* heard or understood, then you will have to develop a great deal of patience and tolerance in order to take responsibility for your desire and not blame another for failing you before you have fully tried. This tolerance is like a meditative discipline in conversation—breathe deeply and calmly return to the subject at hand. Like Ragnell, be confident that you can speak from your knowledge of yourself. If all else fails, simply and sincerely say something like "Those are my needs (or conditions), and when you are ready to talk about them, please let me know."

Being the Subjects of our desires means taking on the challenging, nuanced experience of learning who we are, charting the many layers of our subjective lives, and being accountable for them. Through this process we come to know how we are limited by conditions and happenings beyond our control. As we take responsibility for our own desires, we discover how much we depend on others, and how often we may be mistaken or wrong in wanting certain things. The tolerance we develop for our own mistakes and blind spots spreads out to being tolerant of shortcomings in others, especially those we love.

So how can we claim the validity of our desires without fear of repercussions and shame? How can we use our desires to attain self-knowledge and self-determination, to take responsibility for ourselves and become more authentic in our relations to others? Can we reach a place where our desires no longer drive us and we are content?

Ragnell's story provides us with some preliminary clues, and Diana's death is a cautionary tale. Wanting to be wanted is often a completely hidden desire, confused with wanting to be loved. In order to avoid the temptation to become the Object of Desire, we have to learn to oppose our tendencies to present an image. We must actively claim what we want, even if doing so puts us at risk of being labeled as the hag-bitch. With a confidence in our knowledge, we can firmly and calmly show that we don't fear female desire, that we want to be free from the dominance of appearance and its false power. Until women refuse to live by the belief that female power is beauty, we will be unable to reach the next level of our development, an ability to know and sustain our own truths in all domains of our existence.

The Truth of Being Known

TRUTH IS A WAY OF LIFE, not something that exists outside ourselves. It's being honest and direct and transparent, as well as wholly respectful of those we depend on to sustain us. If our attention is focused on how we look or seem to others, we will find it impossible to know our own hearts. If we become Objects of Desire, we can easily forget how to be Subjects of our own desires. Either we attend to our images, trying to make hidden and implied arrangements for things to go our way, or we attend to our desires and let the chips fall, no matter how we are received.

The Renaissance metaphysician Paracelsus said that we cannot love something without knowing it, or know something without loving it. When we feel deeply loved, we also know that we have been encountered authentically, that we have been true to ourselves in the presence of the other and found that truth fully embraced and accepted. When we tell the truth to a partner or friend, we are indeed vulnerable to being judged, blamed, or rejected. If we hide the truth in favor of protecting ourselves and appearing in a certain way, however, we may retain an illusion of control but we lose the possibility of being known for who we really are, and hence of being loved.

In writing this book it is my goal to illuminate the rocky path from the hidden compulsion to be desired to the responsibility for our own desires, and finally to the knowledge and wisdom that arise from seeing into our limitations and dependence. When we no longer cling to being seen in a particular way and learn to speak the truth with an open heart, we find that almost nothing seems impossible—not because we are in control of everything but because we discover how to depend gratefully on others, how to change when change is required, and, most important, how to be less ashamed, envious, guilty, isolated, and afraid.

TWO

The Menace of Female Beauty

A BEAUTIFUL YOUNG WOMAN symbolizes an almost transcendent power or vitality in our society and others like it. Women feel compelled to imitate her, and men feel compelled to possess her. The refrain *female power is beauty* leads us to believe that possibilities flow directly from our appearances. Thus most American women strive to attain (or torture themselves envying) the image of a pretty, youthful, slender woman.

At a painfully young age an American girl becomes convinced that she exists only in the ways she sees herself reflected. Feelings of liveliness and vitality become connected with the excitement of others: What a pretty girl! What a nice disposition and pleasant manners! She is rewarded for how she appears and not for what she desires or what she produces. Indeed in the past, and even sometimes in the present, female accomplishments (intellectual, professional, athletic) were viewed with embarrassment and accompanied by an apology because girls and women were meant to be powerful not in their actions but only in their appearances.

More often encouraged to evaluate ourselves by our body images than by our actions, we become Objects of Desire. Seeking validation primarily through the interest and excitement reflected back at us by others, we gradually lose sight and control of our own needs, wants, wishes. We become objects even to ourselves, constantly surveying our bodies and our psyches as though from an external point of view. Doubting our own abilities and knowledge, we need reassurance; lacking confidence, we long for flattery. Unable to know ourselves authentically, we want to be wanted instead of loved. We lose track of how it feels to be in charge of our actions and desires. Yet this feels perfectly normal, somehow connected to becoming a woman, because almost everyone else is doing it too.

As historian and author Joan Brumberg says, our problems with appearance are unique to this period. In the past, the question Who am I? was largely answered by the identity "a woman"—broadly constrained and confined by reproductive and social conditions. Now that girls are free to answer the question with a larger range of possibilities—such as artist, scientist, or athlete—they are increasingly naming themselves as an appearance: fat, thin, ugly, pretty. They've learned from a very early age that the power of their gender is tied to what they look like—and how sexy they are—rather than to character or achievement. Brumberg calls this the "body project" and claims that it emanates from middle-class upward strivings, our media-driven culture, and the advice of "experts" on women's power and identity concerns.

There is no way to remain completely free from this message that female power is beauty. As girls and women we live and breathe this atmosphere. It pervades all we do and all the ways we are reflected back to ourselves. In the media there is rarely a female accomplishment that is unaccompanied by a description of what the woman was wearing and/or how she looked. It is as if we must survey a woman's appearance either to find the root of her success in beauty (so she can be reduced to her appearance) or in its absence to explain her success in terms of compensating for her lack of that essential ingredient. For a majority of American women, appearance becomes the central expression of personal identity.

Initial identification with physical appearance happens in adolescence. The obsession with looks and popularity burgeons in girls during the years of beginning self-awareness, between the ages of thirteen and eighteen, when they are developing the capacity to think about themselves, to reflect on their own thoughts and feelings. Just at this time girls are bombarded with images of the desire-awakening maiden.

Girls adjust their motivations and concerns to this identity through dress, mannerisms, activities. Each of us retains the stamp of this original identification within our sense of self and body image for the rest of our lives.

Dissatisfied with Our Images

YET FOR ALL the attention and effort that we direct to bodies and appearances, we are primarily unhappy with them. Two-thirds of all American women, including those who are average-size and thin, believe they are overweight. Americans spend an estimated $5 to $7 billion on weight-loss products that are mostly worthless. The frightening percentages of female dissatisfaction with weight and appearance get younger and larger each year: a recent survey showed that by age thirteen 53 percent of American girls are unhappy with their bodies, and by age seventeen 78 percent are dissatisfied.

Young, educated women are largely dissatisfied with their shapes and sizes, and this unhappiness is linked to fasting, overuse of laxatives (including diuretics), self-induced vomiting, and rigorous exercise. One large survey showed that 61 percent of college women had some type of eating-related problem and that only 33 percent of those questioned reported eating habits that could be considered normal. All these studies point to one thing: body-image dissatisfaction is a fact of life for almost all adolescent and young women.

Many women dislike themselves specifically because they do not meet the standards of our modern-day muses: the supermodels, movie stars, female dancers, and some athletes (gymnasts and skaters, for instance) who weigh between twenty-five and thirty pounds less than the average American woman of the same height. For if female power is beauty, then thinness is the core requirement to be the muse of our time.

Few are immune to our cultural obsession with female thinness. A recent study of 176 women college students showed that those viewing fifty fashion photographs of the "thin ideal" immediately experienced decreased self-esteem and increased self-consciousness, social anxiety, and body dissatisfaction in comparison with those who had not looked at the pictures. Think of how many images of the anorectic woman-child we see in a day—traveling to and from work, glancing at magazines, watching TV. Even women who claimed they did not adhere to an ideal for attractiveness were negatively influenced by seeing the fifty photos. Another recent study showed that just thirty minutes of watching TV programs and advertising can alter a young woman's perception of her body!

Only women over sixty seem to have escaped the thin obsession. According to one study, and in my experience in working with women in psychotherapy, older women are more satisfied with their body images than younger women. Although the researchers could not answer why this was so, they guessed that the crucial difference was that the older women had not been exposed during their adolescence to the widespread influences of the beauty ideal.

Baby boomers like myself, now in our forties and fifties, share with younger women the belief that thinness will lead to power and privileges. We grew up when television and movies were making their imprint on our society. Many of us matched ourselves to female role models from these media, and many of us came to feminism (if we did) with role models like Jane Fonda and Gloria Steinem, who maintained the slender beautiful-woman image alongside claims for greater sovereignty and influence. My teenage years were influenced by dieting when it was seen almost as a prerequisite to being grown-up. Baby boomers may be feminists and have successful public lives, but often we feel the confusion of beauty bondage almost as acutely as our younger counterparts, whose images may be honed by Kate Moss rather than Jane Fonda.

My forty-something client Anne feels trapped and disempowered by her body image. She is full-bodied and athletic, well-presented and fashionable, but Anne doesn't like either her weight or her body. "I know it's wrong that I get so preoccupied with my weight. The truth is that I feel more powerful, even kind of cocky, when I'm at my thinnest. But I always gain back those extra five or ten pounds—and they increase a little each time I gain them back—and then I feel so negative about my appearance that it interferes with almost everything."

On a few occasions I suggested to Anne that she experiment with eating just what she wanted and see what would happen. She responded with fear in her voice. "I really couldn't ever do that, because I would be afraid that I would keep on eating. It's like I have a hole inside that I want to fill up with food."

Why Skinny Looks Powerful

POWER AND INFLUENCE have always been promised to the desire-awakening maiden, but why is our modern-day muse an anorectic woman-child, so thin as to make us wince? When I call her anorectic, I am both describing her appearance and hoping to shock you, for among the physical and psychological dangers of female beauty, our obsession with weight is probably the greatest.

The writer Laura Fraser believes that being thin offers an illusion of control. In our chaotic lives, our efforts to control our weight seem to promise control of other things: "Being thin sends a visual message to the world . . . that a woman works hard at being attractive, and is therefore good at her traditional job of being a desirable sexual object, romantic partner and consumer. By being lean, she also conveys the idea that she's disciplined, efficient, and in control of herself." Women who suffer from eating disorders, who starve themselves in physically devastating anorexia or "purge" themselves of unwanted calories through vomiting or laxatives, defend their practices with an air of superiority, often saying openly, "Doesn't *everyone* want to be thin?" These women know that control of the body feels like power, and they won't surrender this feeling for any promise of health or normalcy—often until they are very sick or almost dead.

From surveys and studies we know that people do indeed connect thinness with control and competence, but the illusion of control has always been an aspect of female beauty bondage. The aura of influence and power linked to the muse has in earlier periods been described in terms of skin, breasts, hair, eyes, waist, and voice. In other words, thinness is only her current guise.

Fraser traces the history of female thinness to a change in women's roles. The earlier image of a woman as "pleasingly plump" or roundly sensual emphasized her maternal potential. But changes in women's lives and aspirations, coming with suffrage and greater athletic freedom, also brought a new self-conscious awareness of the female body.

Swimming and bicycling in the early part of this century brought women's legs into the open, and the new consumer culture began to set standards for how legs should look. By the 1920s the plumper figure had given way to the straight, slender flapper image. Hidden beneath the cultural message of the greater freedom of the twenties was the dictate of restraint in maintaining a slender female body.

By the 1920s manufacturers and advertisers had begun to see women primarily as consumers. Beauty and body products were invented, and smoking was advocated as a way to stay thin. This consumerism was offered as a new freedom, but it was hardly liberating, because advertisements increasingly spoke to women's anxieties, self-consciousness, and fears about themselves. With the advent of the birth-control pill, greater freedom from pregnancies and lactation, and the lengthened time between menarche and menopause, it was possible to bring more and more control to female appearance—especially weight.

Gradually what emerged as a beauty ideal was a body type that resembled more a man's than a woman's body—little or no fat, muscles showing through the skin, and an angular face, legs, and arms. This body image is almost impossible to maintain without an eating disorder; it is unrealistic to aspire to it and have a healthy existence. The icons of this anorectic woman-child, the supermodels, often live lives that are crazed with drugs, starvation, abusive relationships, and celebrity. These women are the role models for a coming generation of girls who, according to a large survey of third-graders, would choose a career as a famous fashion model over being president. Models' power—earning capacity, social status, media attention—communicates an ideal of control that is being internalized by girls and young women in place of an understanding of their own desires and self-determination.

But we cannot blame just the media for indoctrinating our young girls with the desire to be thin. Many of us are unwittingly lending a hand. When Anne talks to her teenage daughter about issues of female appearance, she is so ashamed of her own preoccupations that she misleads her daughter. While she might tell her daughter about feminism, achievement, competence, career, and creativity—and mix this with rich accounts of being a mother and a wife—she does not discuss what Laura Fraser calls her "third job": staying thin. Instead Anne encourages her daughter, as most of us do, not to put too much emphasis on appearance. "Don't worry about that, it will take care of itself; you look just fine."

But Anne's daughter notices her mother going from gym to spa, from cosmetic counter to hair salon. She is right to challenge her mother: "If appearance is not important, why do you spend so much time on yours? You, especially, you're a *feminist*." Anne's daughter will doubt the usefulness of her mother's feminism if her mother cannot answer questions about these concerns. But Anne cannot speak directly to this issue because she has not been able to take responsibility for her own desire to be thin. She hasn't been able to say that she's afraid of being overlooked if she doesn't work on her appearance. She hasn't been able to tell her daughter how sordid this chapter of female appearance has been in the recent history of feminism.

Our forebears may have constrained the female body with girdles and corsets, but the feminist era has marketed the female body as a power product that must be kept thin and under internal control. Feminists have encouraged women to claim their power, but they have not taught them how to distinguish male fantasies of the desire-awakening maiden from authentic sources of female power. The image of the anorectic woman-child appears to girls and young women to be a viable means to success in a feminist-influenced world.

The belief that we must be thin in order to be successful results in feelings of insecurity about ourselves and our abilities. Obsessive control of the female body leads not to power but to shame, self-consciousness, confusion, illness, even death by eating disorders. Longing to be reassured of our worth and validity, we submit to humiliating advice from experts who tell us what and when to eat, and how to exercise, as if we were children. Most women who are convinced that they are fat are, in fact, no more than fifteen to forty pounds over the social standards for what is desirable in the female body image. Studies have proven that this margin makes no real difference to health or longevity.

If we want to be more self-determining and responsible, we must become acutely aware of how images of female beauty are used against us. The camera may not steal our souls, but it commercializes and markets our bodies. Mirrors and cameras have left us with an insidious and pervasive obsession with thinness in place of recognition and knowledge of our own desires.

Men under the Spell

MEN, TOO, LIVE with the consequences of the belief that female power is beauty. They are often preoccupied with the goal of attracting and possessing a slender, beautiful woman as the means of proving their masculinity or personal attractiveness, or simply because they believe such a woman would enliven and complete them. More than forty years ago feminist author Simone de Beauvoir reminded us that when men set themselves up as free beings, as Subjects of their own desires, they needed a contrast or a negation of that freedom. Thus the attractive woman became a necessity in men's lives. "Man aspires to clothe in his own dignity whatever he conquers and possesses," de Beauvoir wrote, so he allows the beautiful woman to retain "a little of her primitive magic" while she shares in his dignity by becoming his possession. The desire-awakening maiden is assumed, by men, to have a magic of her own in being the Object of Desire.

But while men might want to possess the muse, they also fear her influence. Even a two-dimensional image of a woman of a certain age and shape can dumbfound a man. Advertisers drape a skinny model across a car hood, dangle a cigarette from her fingers, or pose her bikini-clad body alongside the pool of an expensive resort knowing that the promise men read in her eyes compels them to purchase. Men often report serious distrust, of both women and other men, from living in an atmosphere where they are expected to compete for the most beautiful woman, a scenario represented in countless myths, the battle over Helen of Troy probably being the most famous.

The primitive magic of the desire-awakening maiden turns man against man and can confuse an individual's judgment. Rape may be an "inevitable outcome," say certain sociobiologists, as male sexual arousal is assumed to be controlled by female appearance. Only the strongest of men will succeed in capturing the muse, benefiting future generations through the pairing of strength and beauty, according to this account. Genetic ideologues such as Richard Dawkins and E. O. Wilson claim that beautiful women are powerful *because* strong men want to possess them.

In other words, male dominance is intrinsic to the power of female beauty; the muse has no legitimate power and knowledge of her own. The refrain *female power is beauty* creates a condition in which women can never be free from male standards for appearance and behavior. Male desire and fantasy dictate the contours of the female Object of Desire while her powers over men's reason and judgment are despised and ridiculed. Bondage to her appearance leaves her needing reassurance and flattery, wanting to be wanted instead of loved, and empowers male desires and male images of female beauty and worth. Meanwhile, hatred and control of the female body come, as we shall see, from male fantasies of women and their dangerous powers.

Pandora and the Curse of Female Beauty

THE STORY OF the first woman in Greek mythology lays bare the meaning of Woman in patriarchy, telling us how and why the beautiful female must be under the control of powerful men. Sadly enough, this story is as relevant to our culture today as it was centuries ago.

Accounts of Pandora go back to the eighth century B.C.E. and the Greek poet Hesiod, although the story has been told and retold in many forms. We possess what is probably only a short fragment of a much longer tale, but it is all that remains. My account is paraphrased from the two versions of Hesiod.

PANDORA

Once upon a time there was great rivalry between the gods and men. Prometheus, the champion of mankind, had stolen the power of fire and brought it to earth. When Zeus saw the flames flickering below him, he fell into a deadly fury.

In retaliation Zeus plotted to bring a terrible evil to men that would be equal to the boon of fire. He commanded a lowly god, a master craftsman, to fashion the image of a desire-awakening maiden. Mixing earth and water, the craftsman gave his creation a face as beautiful as those of the immortal goddesses, and a voice and strength of her own. Then he was aided by the goddesses themselves: one taught the maiden womanly crafts, while another gave her a radiance of charm and seduction.

When this first woman was fully formed, Zeus commanded Hermes, a trickster by nature, to fill the maiden with bitchy shamelessness and lies. Hermes made sure that the maiden had flatteries and treacheries in place of a heart; then he commanded her to speak. Other gods and goddesses adorned her with golden necklaces and wreaths of spring flowers. Hermes named her Pandora, which means "rich in gifts," because she had been given so many gifts by the gods, and because she was a "gift" to men.

Zeus sent Pandora to earth by way of Epimetheus, whose name means "he who learns only from experience." He was to deliver her and leave no suspicion of the trickery involved. Epimetheus accepted Pandora as a gift to men and presented her to them as the first woman.

Shortly after Pandora's arrival on earth, her curiosity led her to discover a great clay vessel that was stored underground. The vessel, containing sicknesses and evils and death itself, had been buried explicitly to protect men from harm. Pandora opened this jar and let out into the world all sufferings and evils, including death—the great divider between humans and gods. Only hope remained, kept in unbreakable captivity according to the will of Zeus.

Thus, Zeus was triumphant. By his "gift" of woman, he punished men with an evil that was equal to fire. Beautiful but empty, Pandora was the first female of Western culture to prac- tice her wiles against innocent, defenseless men. And so began the influence of woman in the lives of men.

THE GREEK STORY of Pandora reveals the template for the female Object of Desire—empty of her own desires and filled with seductive powers. Her deceptions, treacheries, and flatter- ies can defeat male power. She is vindictive and manipulative, and she was created specifically as a punishment to men. Like that other first woman, Eve (whose story may have been taken from Pandora's), she is the embodiment of evil.

So we begin to see how and why the desire-awakening maiden is cursed by her beauty: since she is judged to be empty, she must be dominated and controlled. Without a heart, she lacks a truth and nature of her own. In their absence, she may want to take possession of everything. She may want to have not only what she wants but also to control and domi-nate what men have.

For after men have dreamed up their muse, they dread the lack of control they feel in her presence. Ancient religious laws and moral codes warn against her evil powers. A beautiful woman is evil because she possesses a power over men's reason and judgment. Yet that power is present only when men see it. It has to do not with the woman herself but only with how she is seen by others. *Female power is beauty* can never be free from male standards because men consciously and unconsciously shape the image of their Object of Desire.

Woman can aspire to share in Man's dignity by being his companion if she can become his Object, but she cannot share in his power because she has nothing of her own to offer. Her power—a beautiful appearance—depends on his reflection, and her destiny remains in his control.

The Double Bind of Female Beauty

IDENTIFYING WITH PANDORA—evil perhaps but also desirable, slender, young—may still seem preferable to being seen as the lonely hag, ugly and ashamed. Beautiful is arousing, vitalizing, exciting, and ugly is old, devitalizing, boring. The muse enhances life, and the hag snuffs it out. Yet, as we have seen, the muse exists only as an aspect of male power and dom-inance. Her powers to vitalize are to be used for someone else, not for herself.

In the last chapter I discussed the link between shame and emptiness in the monstrous power of the hag. You'll recall that the shameful self is empty of anything good; it is bad and inferior. Just as the hag living in the woods is an image of shame linked to women who identify with being monstrous or poisonous, the heartless muse is an image of shame linked to women who identify with being only an appearance, the desire-awakening maiden. When we identify with the muse, we are constantly troubled by obsessions about appearance, fears of aging, shame, dissatisfaction, confusion, and ignorance of our own desires. Beautiful women must meet the standards for the muse; today they are not even free to eat.

Whether we fear to be seen as the hag or desire to be seen as the muse, we are trapped in the double bind of female beauty: damned if we are ugly and damned if we are beautiful. Within this pervasive double bind we are restless and unsure, needing the affirmation of others. For many women, as we saw, identity *is* appearance, so everything is tied to approval and attention. Princess Diana was a perfect example of a woman trapped in beauty bondage. Although she complained about photographers haunting her, she also openly complied with the media and used them to her advantage. The biographer Donald Spoto says that Diana was frequently a "willing victim," and he describes her as "a young woman who desperately needed to feel wanted . . . and according to the ethos of modern life, nothing so confirms self-esteem as media attention. Diana Spencer was receiving . . . the attention from the press that she needed in order to feel alive and valuable."

Many of us are stuck in beauty bondage because we are too afraid of being seen as the hag if we find freedom and comfort in our own bodies. Unless our thighs are toned, our breasts perky, our skin smooth, we are not wanted. Just as we inadvertently confirm suspicions that an emotionally demanding woman is a monster, we confirm that freedom of appearance leads to loneliness and isolation when we bring our appearance

under obsessive control. Liberation from the bind is often eas-
ier for a woman who has felt herself to be the hag than for one
who has seen herself as the muse. The hag, after all, has never
fully surrendered access to her own desires, even though she
may be ashamed of her body. When she comes out of the
woods, as Ragnell showed us, she knows what she wants and is
unafraid to say it.

To step outside the double bind, we have to confront the
hag in ourselves: the image of an overpowering female whose
needs and desires are monstrous. Both she and the heartless
muse are fantasies of male dominance that are used to keep
women disempowered. Trapped in the double bind of female
beauty, we have identified with these images, bringing shame
and defeat to ourselves.

The Muse and the Slut

MANY OF US, no matter how feminist we are, join with men
in reducing women to their appearances, dividing women
among themselves through competition, jealousy, envy of
physical traits. Believing that female power is beauty, we live
off each other's images in crass and painful comparisons of
thighs, stomachs, hips, breasts, wrinkles, and hair. We use
images of women to stand in place of understanding their
desires and meanings; we go along with the Pandora story by
acting as though a woman is her appearance and is empty of a
heart.

Such is the story of Monica Lewinsky, the notorious twenty-
something intern at the White House. Lewinsky engaged in
oral sex in the Oval Office in exchange (we assume) for being
desired by the President of the United States. Her story stirs

our contemporary Pandora imaginings. Men and women have described Lewinsky as a "bimbo"—pretty but empty—and even as a "slut" who uses her seductive powers to her own advantage. How does the muse turn into a slut?

On television and in all sorts of media, Lewinsky has been characterized by aspects of her appearance that fall outside cultural standards for female beauty (usually in terms of being chubby or overweight) and by her seductiveness (in terms of her behaviors with the president, former lovers, and boyfriends). Reported accounts of her personality and appearance imply that she is just "too much"—too pushy, too flashy, too needy, too flirtatious, too inquisitive.

Feminist commentators have remarked that many women, even feminists, do not champion her cause because Lewinsky represents the "other woman," the "young thing" at the office or the workplace, who threatens to seduce our husbands or boyfriends. Within the double bind of female beauty, we encourage girls to become these flirty creatures, then condemn them for the power they supposedly have over men.

The slut is the muse metamorphosed into the hag-bitch. Within the double bind of female beauty, the heartless Pandora works her wiles on innocent men. If she intrudes on male power in some manner that interferes with the ordinary "rules of the game"—as patriarchy has set up rules to protect male power—then she becomes the monstrous hag. Women, especially, are often keen to show that the slut is not attractive. She is too fat, wears too much makeup, is too loud. In other words, she has become the hag who dominates men and children with her magical powers.

So the woman who competes to be the Object of Desire is labeled not only by men but by other women. But calling other women (or ourselves) sluts and bimbos is just another symptom of the shaming of female desire, seeing ourselves and our needs as monstrous or manipulative or overpowering.

How can we escape this double bind? The answer seems clear: we must let go of our beauty fixation. We must stop identifying who we are by how we look. And we must learn to protect ourselves against harmful stereotypes about female appearance by recognizing how they undo our power and undermine our self-esteem.

Enjoyment of our bodies, pleasurable exercise, and healthy eating are the means to long life and good health. But these restorative attitudes and activities can only arise from knowledge of ourselves as Subjects of our own desires. As long as we fear the emotional power of the hag, we will direct our attention and interests to appearances rather than to pleasure and enjoyment.

Becoming Subjects of Appearance

WHEN I WAS A TEENAGER I was faced with a dilemma. As a young girl I was chubby and wore thick glasses. I saw myself as a good girl and an achiever, not someone who could be pretty or popular. But when I was sixteen my fate suddenly changed: I was allowed to have contact lenses. Even though I was far from being the muse type of my generation (busty, slim hips and ankles, long, straight hair), after I got my contacts the popular boys, who previously hadn't given me the time of day, suddenly greeted me by name. The choice presented itself for the first time: appearance or achievement.

Intuitively I knew these were distinct domains, in which the rules were different. If I wanted to compete for female beauty, I could no longer be number one in my class. Instead of speaking up, I would have to develop mannerisms designed to hide what I knew so that I wouldn't challenge the boys.

Already I had had too much fun with achievement; I couldn't imagine giving up my own desires in order to appear in a certain way. So I chose the path of achievement—but tried very hard to be attractive, too.

I'm still fighting the battle. I sometimes hide from myself the meaning of my daily exercise, as though it had nothing to do with my appearance. I tell myself (and others) that I exercise for my health, yet I know that the exercise has a compulsive edge that compensates for fears about appearance and aging. But at an early age I learned not to bank on my appearance, and in so doing I gained certain freedoms. I retained a strong sense of self-determination and a belief that I was in charge of my life. I tried to claim directly what I wanted. But the consequences were not always positive: I often was left out, lonely, ignorant of feminine social protocols—ways in which women are expected to be self-effacing, indirect, invisible, especially in the bailiwicks of male power. I never learned how to keep my mouth shut, as my mother, my daughter, and my husband have frequently reminded me. So I have been labeled the hag-bitch, and I have learned to cope with it. I have learned the lesson of Ragnell: be calm, breathe deeply, restate my aims, don't blame, and, most of all, don't feel ashamed of my desires.

Although I have not been immune to beauty standards, I have elected to identify myself with something other than my appearance. I can step outside the double bind of female beauty, knowing I am neither the dreaded hag nor the dangerous muse. I look for role models of women who do not identify with the muse, who are often labeled as the hag in some form but seem truly indifferent to it: historic figures like Eleanor Roosevelt, Golda Meir, and Shirley Chisholm, who spoke their minds without seeming to fuss about their reputations. Contemporary women like Attorney General Janet Reno and writers Carolyn Heilbrun, Nancy Mairs, and Joyce Carol Oates are also exemplary; they are honest, open, fallible, and outside the double bind of female beauty. Many black women have been role models for me; among the most famous writers are some of my favorites: bell hooks, Maya Angelou, Toni Morrison. They're irresistible as clear, powerful women who seem free from false images that arise from male imagination.

Taking responsibility for stepping outside the double bind of female beauty is not easy or straightforward. Because we *are* evaluated by our appearance, we must be willing to change our own evaluations while withstanding others' and to bring our hidden desires into the light. Only by opposing appearance standards in our own talk and self-talk can we gradually change the cultural conversations and symbols. We are like Ragnell coming out of the woods to tell the truth: we want sovereignty over our appearance and identity.

To become the Subject of your own desires, you, too, must resist the double bind of female beauty. In order to resist it, first you must be able to identify it, and be alert when it is implied in people's observations and actions. Every one of us is up against a struggle not to identify with being the negative hag-bitch because we refuse to be stereotyped and constrained by male fantasies of women's power.

To be Subjects of our appearance, we must experiment and enjoy. Rather than being slaves to fashion, we should use color and fabric and body contours to express our pleasures and desires in individual ways. Drawing on our imaginations to come up with appearances and styles to satisfy us in expressing ourselves in the various domains of our lives, we can move outside the dictates of our skinny cultural muse. Most important, clothing, makeup, and public demeanor must no longer be translated automatically so that patriarchal stereotypes abound: the fact that she's wearing bib overalls does not mean she's a lesbian. The fact that she doesn't shave her legs does not mean she's a feminist. The fact that she's wearing panty hose does not mean she's a housewife. The fact that she's decorated with makeup and jewelry does not mean she's "cheap" or some other version of slut. The fact that she's wearing high heels does not mean she wants men to look at her legs. As many black women have taught me, dressing *up* means getting bigger, more colorful, more dramatic—more powerful—and sometimes high heels help. Being alert to the many, varied ways that women can dress and be and act ensures that we do not automatically see a woman's expression of herself as a sign of a pat identity according to patriarchal rules.

As we engage with others and ourselves in domains outside the double bind of female beauty, we will learn and develop new ways of seeing and new images of being female. Until we experiment in these ways, it will be impossible to oppose the machinery that supports the industry of female beauty bondage. No doubt it is useful to reveal the profits and meanings of these markets, and no doubt it is critically important to understand the history and development of female appearance as an aspect of male dominance. But only when we are able to change our own attitudes will we be strong enough to oppose the culture around us and liberate our appearances from the dictates of male power.

Pandora as Subject of Desire

LET US LOOK once again at the story of Pandora. When Pandora dug up the sealed earthenware jar, she uncovered the buried troubles and miseries of human life. Most important, she let death out into the world. Death is at the core of the name given to humans by the Greeks: the mortals, those who will die. Different from other species, humans are aware of their own deaths. Our mortality should remind us of our limitation and impermanence. Pandora as Subject followed her curiosity and created humans as mortals, living with a knowledge of their own limitations.

I like to imagine that Pandora was looking for her heart, the lost meaning that would be her truth. Feeling her own emptiness, she was curious, and her curiosity eventually led her to dig up the hidden miseries of human life. Perhaps she dug up the buried remains from the mythical matriarchal goddesses, such as Demeter and Persephone and Gaia, who preceded the Greek pantheon at Olympus—remains that had been transformed into misery and trouble by being left out and denied by the newer patriarchal gods. Thus, we could say that the limitation of death and illness Pandora brought to men was also a limitation on their patriarchal power, their habits of and inclinations for controlling through dominance and aggression.

The Truth about Female Beauty

THE HEART AND TRUTH about female beauty is that it has been under the dominion of male power and fantasy for far too long. It has produced all kinds of suffering and misery. But to free female appearance from male dominion means to open up what has been hidden. Following Pandora's lead, we realize that the only cure for shame is to bring our buried meanings and feelings into the light of day. Many of these concern our fears about our failings, ugliness, inferiority.

Pandora seen from this perspective exposes us to the knowledge of our limitations. Because we are always vulnerable to conditions beyond our control—illness, loss, death—that escaped the earthenware jar, we wish for a perfection that we cannot achieve. Our own ideals can cause us unending anguish if they lead us to believe that the world should go as we would like it to. We humans have limited power, but we *are* responsible for our intentions, thoughts, desires, and actions. Pandora liberates us to understand and work within the constraints of being human. The hope that remains is the hope that we will learn from our limitations.

In Chapter One, I talked about Jung's theory of psychological complexes and how our old emotional habits get in the way of being able to change our attitudes, identities, and actions. Pandora shows us something about changing the psychological complexes surrounding the meaning of female appearance.

The old habits of patriarchal societies deem women's appearance to be their greatest power. These habits promote fear and shame when our appearance doesn't match the image of the muse. They produce envy, rivalry, bitterness, and isolation among women themselves, who compete for the prizes of female beauty under male dominance. But the beautiful Woman of patriarchy is the symbol of male power. Her legacy is about power between and among men, not about real and actual power of and for women.

For us to act as Subjects of our desires, we have to bring into the light our own hidden intentions and attitudes in order to stop judging people (including ourselves) by appearance. No amount of feminist analysis will dissolve the belief that female power is beauty until we can stop perpetuating it. Only women can change such beliefs, and we will do that one by one, as we come to understand the destructive false power of images of female beauty under male control.

THREE

Sex through the Looking Glass

THE "LOOKING GLASS" of female appearance is the surface that reflects our desire to be desirable. To travel *through* it is to encounter a hidden underworld of female sexual shame, embarrassment, confusion, frustration, and numbness. Wanting to be wanted leads to little pleasure in sexual passion or union. Instead of discovering and developing practices and routines of female sexual pleasure, women want to be admired and claimed for their seductive charms and beauty. Our obsession with our physical appearance prohibits or interferes with our capacities for sexual passion and merger. And those who believe they have failed at the appearance game, and identify with the negative hag, disconnect from their sexual desires through resentment and loneliness. Damned if you're beautiful and damned if you're not, the double bind of female beauty has meant a widespread, painful loss of female sexual desire through excessive concern about appearance and the shame of self-loathing.

Nothing dampens sexual pleasure more than self-consciousness. Nothing increases self-consciousness as much as excessive concern about appearance and desirability. To feel deeply aroused and engaged with our sexual passions, we have to temporarily be taken over by the experience of the moment. In sex this feels like a loss of our ordinary boundaries, the loss of me versus you, of in-here versus out-there. As Otto Kernberg, a well-known psychoanalyst, writes, sexual passion is "crossing the boundaries of the self" or "merging with the other" in a way that paradoxically still allows us to feel a separate identity. This kind of sexual merger is impossible if you're caught up in fears about the size or shape of parts of your face or body, or are in constant anxiety about being rejected.

Any passion demands the courage to enter into a desired state or event in the face of dangers; in sex, we fear being engulfed by the other's needs or crushed by the other's lack of response, rejection, or abandonment. Mature sexual love dissolves anxieties and fears of engulfment or abandonment through repeated experiences of pleasure, joy, and transcendence in passionate sexual merger. To enter into and sustain such passion requires more than desire to be with another. It requires at least a modicum of ease with one's own physical and emotional being, liking oneself well enough to want to share oneself intimately with another.

The double bind of female beauty, which engenders acute self-consciousness, may explain why many women have a hard time believing that sexual pleasures could be easily accessible to them. Most national surveys of sexuality and sexual desire show that American women—whether married, cohabiting, or single—want sex less often than men, experience orgasm less often, and find greater satisfaction in emotional intimacy than in genital sex. Researchers report that women equate sexual satisfaction with emotional closeness, while men equate sexual satisfaction with physical sex. This difference between women and men appears to transcend race, class, and education.

From these findings and the stereotypes that abound in our culture, we might come to believe that sexual desire is simply more a man's than a woman's. After all, men have sex more often, fantasize about sex more, have more orgasms and more sexual partners than women have. Also, women in lesbian relationships have genital sex less often than women in heterosexual relationships—a finding that has been used, even by some lesbian researchers, to argue that genital sexual pleasure may be the expression of male, not female, desire. If lesbians don't express much desire for genital sex, then it seems that when women are left to their own devices, they simply don't need or want much sex.

Pleasure and Desire

IN A BOOK that I wrote about couples, *You're Not What I Expected*, I commented on the popular notion that women want emotional intimacy more than men, and men want physical sex more than women. From pop psychology experts, we hear that women "want intimacy in order to be sexual" and men "want sex in order to be intimate." But it seemed to me then—and studies have now confirmed—that women had not had enough pleasure in sex in order to want more. Desire is present only when something that has been pleasurable or gratifying in the past is now missing.

To use an example I provided in my earlier book: if you hear about a wonderful, exotic Colombian yam—about its color, taste, and consistency—you may long to try it, but you cannot desire it until you have tasted it. Confronted with a dessert menu and the choice of this exotic yam over a well-loved dessert, you would probably choose your favorite dessert. In any case, you wouldn't salivate over the yam until you had tasted it, and liked it. If you haven't tasted the pleasure, then you won't feel the desire. Thus many more women than men lack sexual desire because female sexual experience has not been reliably pleasurable.

Perhaps you, like so many of us, have found the widespread lack of female sexual pleasure confusing because, ideally, women can have multiple orgasms and sustain arousal for very long periods. But from recent research on American couples, I have come to understand that women rarely believe that their *lack of pleasure* is the problem. Instead, they feel guilty about their lack of desire. They feel blamed (and blame themselves) for not wanting more sex, and eventually they are angry and resentful that their partners want them to desire sex.

Like many of the sex researchers, I believe that the lack of female desire is a cultural condition, not a biological destiny. It seems to me to be related to definitions of "femininity" that began to emerge in the nineteenth century. When "feminine" was equated with nature (as a passive force) and "masculine" with culture (as an active force), women began to be widely regarded as Objects who would receive the desires and interests of others but have none of their own.

By the end of the nineteenth century, women were advised to be sexually passive as wives—sometimes even fully clothed during intercourse—because doctors and theologians defined the sex act primarily as the expression of male orgasm in the service of procreation. If men wanted sex purely for pleasure, often they pursued it outside their marriages, especially with prostitutes. Men were to be Subjects and women were to be Objects of sexual passion, and this was all considered natural—biologically and theologically destined. Women's ignorance of their own sexual pleasures, their forced confinement to domesticity and children, and their later preoccupations with physical appearance have all contributed to shutting down female sexual desire over the past two centuries.

But what of earlier periods of time? In her book *Promiscuities*, Naomi Wolf writes at length about the history of female sexual desire in Western cultures. Beginning in the sixteenth century, there are records of female sexual pleasure being "scientifically" studied. A Venetian scientist, Renaldus Columbus, called the clitoris the "seat of woman's delight" and provided a detailed description of orgasm through manipulation of it. Because of women's extensive possibilities for sustained sexual pleasure, they were often described as the more sexually driven of the two sexes. Physicians and midwives recommended sensitive and thorough stimulation of the clitoris on all occasions of lovemaking, especially as incentive and preparation for conception, as a way to satisfy female sexual desire so that women would not become agitated and restless in a state of unsatisfied desire (the image we now have of men). Women's sexual capacity was heralded and feared; if women were sexually insatiable, how could they be possessed and controlled by one man?

Gradually, the belief that men have the greater sex drive countered earlier theories. Increasingly women were expected to be confined at home with children and to fill roles that left them on the margins of society. Around the end of the eighteenth century, according to Wolf, experts shifted their attention from an emphasis on female sexual needs to a focus on the tender affection that mothers give their children. Women began to be idealized in terms of endearment for reasons that were economic and political.

The nineteenth- and twentieth-century sexual ideology claimed that women were better equipped than men to bring their sexual impulses and desires under control because women were natural caregivers in being mothers. By the middle and end of the nineteenth century, doctors and scientists widely counseled that rampant sexual desire in a woman could lead her to hysteria, criminal acts, and violence. Cultural standards shifted to purity in women as they were increasingly expected to submit to their husbands' desires and to domestic routines. By the early part of the twentieth century, the female counterpart to the male sex drive had become the "maternal instinct."

At the turn of the twenty-first century, we still believe that women's sexual expression is tied more to emotional closeness than to sexual pleasure. Although many women would reject the idea that they are programmed with a maternal instinct, they describe their intimacy needs in terms of tenderness, affection, and closeness rather than sexual pleasure. In a recent study of female sexual desire, the researchers summarize their findings in saying that men and women engage in sex "for different reasons; men are more motivated by physical pleasure and women are desirous of expressing emotion." Neither the number of orgasms nor the amount of pleasure in sexual activities was as important to the women as their perceptions of how emotionally close the relationship was.

No doubt this emotional closeness is a prerequisite to a deeply satisfying sexual union, but it is not more than a prerequisite. Without the reliable pleasure of arousal and transcendence through orgasm, women do not have access to the experience of a mature passionate love that could awaken, again and again, their sexual desire. On the contrary, the same study discovered that women in physically abusive relationships were having sexual intercourse *more* often than women in nonabusive relationships. As the researchers say, "The relationship between female sexual desire and how often a woman engages in sex is likely to be mediated by her husband." In other words, in abusive relationships the husband uses sex as a means of power over his partner, and his insistence on having sex is greater than the insistence of husbands in nonabusive relationships.

This last illustration makes clear an underlying power dynamic in the lack of female sexual desire. If sexual encounters and activities are assumed by a woman to satisfy male sexual desire—if men are Subjects and women are Objects—then a self-determining woman might not want to engage in sex. Furthermore, most of the images of the sexual woman in our society are shaped by male fantasies of the slut, bimbo, dominatrix. Amidst these images a self-determining woman will hold on to her own power by resisting engagement in sex for someone else's pleasure. She will refuse to have sexual relations with any partner unless she wants to. And because sex hasn't been pleasurable enough for them to create desire, most self-determining women won't initiate sex very often because they have not discovered their own pleasure in it. Reliable female sexual pleasure (even between two women) remains elusive. In this period of feminism many mature women feel freer to say No to sex, but they are not free to find Yes.

The Seduction of Power

INSTEAD OF WONDERING about and investigating the absence of sexual pleasure, many women unknowingly believe that the *seduction of power* can substitute for sexual pleasures. By this I mean a feeling of control over one's own body paired with a feeling of triumph over male sexual desire, both in arousing it and in being able to decline it if one so desires. The seduction of power may include having no sex at all *or* engaging in risky sex—but clearly one has power over sex.

Feeling sexy, attracting attention, and wanting to be wanted become the goals, even though sex may initially feel like an exciting by-product of the attention. We tune in to what effect we are having in sex rather than to what we want in terms of our own needs and pleasures.

The desire to be reflected through the looking glass of someone else's desire is based on the felt experience that female power lies outside of oneself and must be attracted and won. Instead of practicing power within ourselves, we seek it by controlling another's responses. We come to see ourselves only as reflected in our lovers' eyes. But we cannot fill our own needs with another's desires. Trapped in these sex and power games, we become acutely self-conscious.

In place of developing our own erotic lives, we become obsessed about appearance, immersed in images of ugly-beautiful, and distracted by self-conscious emotions, such as shame, embarrassment, envy, or jealousy. We don't investigate what is beneath the surface; instead we feel betrayed by how little sexual desire we find in ourselves, blaming either ourselves or our partners. Unknowingly we are bound up in the psychological complex of muse or hag, accompanied by fantasies about others desiring or despising us. As in female beauty bondage, identifying with the muse or the hag makes us vulnerable to internalizing men's fears and fantasies about us. Trapped in the double bind of beauty, we are limited in our awareness of pleasure for the sake of pleasure.

Linda is in her late twenties and comes to psychotherapy because of her low self-esteem. She has had a series of uncommitted sexual and emotional relationships with both men and women, but in no way does she show any concern about her lack of commitment. She says that "love is a false god and we should all be practical about what we can and cannot have. No one else can really make us happy, so we shouldn't have to commit to someone else for life."

Linda is afraid to have children because she worries that her fragile personality would break down under the weight. Sometimes she believes she should become celibate as a way to avoid the pain she feels when she loses a lover. When a sexual relationship ends Linda feels dead and afraid of being alone, and even when she begins a new relationship, she is suspicious that her partner will disappoint her terribly in the end.

Linda feels alive and vital only when she believes that someone else finds her sexy and exciting. At even the slightest withdrawal on the part of her lover, she becomes anxious and begins to suspect that she is unwanted. Since she is afraid of being rejected, she often cuts off relationships prematurely, just as they have become a bit real, a bit beyond fantasy. She knows little about her own desires except to say that she has a "sex and love addiction." This knowledge addresses only her symptoms.

The Meaner Face of Desire

LINDA IS MOTIVATED by a hidden desire: she wants to be wanted. As we've learned, when our desires are hidden or unknown to us, they take over much of our emotional lives—often as part of an unconscious psychological complex that promotes certain images and impulses, such as the desire-awakening maiden or the soul-sucking hag.

When Linda has sex with a lover, she becomes absorbed in whether or not her partner finds her attractive and exciting. She is excited only by her partner's excitement. If her partner is worrying about Linda's pleasure (will she have an orgasm? will she be responsive? and so on), then both are distracted and off-center. Linda is worried about whether or not her partner is aroused (is she or he bored? is she or he turned off somehow by my body? is she or he tired of me?), and her partner is worried about *Linda's* pleasure and desire. Rather than engaging in authentic passion, they are making arrangements—conscious or hidden—to secure the responses they want. These forced arrangements (from evoking to demanding a response from the other) usually require us to act out cultural stereotypes of the desire-awakening maiden and her master (or vice versa in today's sadomasochistic "scenes"). Under these conditions both women and men confuse love and power, and miss the opportunity for deepened pleasure and passion.

In heterosexual sex—especially outside an intimate rela-tionship—men can easily be drawn into fantasies and actions of conquest and dominance of the female body. They want to possess the fantasied power of the female body for themselves, and they may feel humiliated when it is refused to them. As

I've noted, possessing a beautiful woman is a sign of power among men. Winning the seductive woman reinforces masculine identity in a world where men compete for the desire-awakening maiden. Once a woman is ostensibly his, a man may feel especially shamed by sexual refusal and rejection from his partner. For many men sexual rejection feels humiliating because they are exposed in their visible sexual arousal and vulnerable to being teased and subdued.

Women also want the power of having an erotic effect. This is a meaner face of female desire—the craving to have power over another's sexual responses, the need to be filled up with someone else's desire. This seduction of power confuses eros—the desire for connection—with influence or power.

Sex and love are easily corrupted by power struggles over the female body. If a female partner wants to be dominated or possessed as a sign that she is alluring (or she wants to dominate her partner for the same effect) while her male partner wants her to express an orgasm so that he is certain she is satisfied, both are distracted in their attempts to command the female body.

In a mature partnership there is room for all sorts of sexual fantasies—for aggressive longings and roles—provided they are blended into a loving relationship in which the partners are capable of understanding themselves and respecting each other. To know your own pleasures and fantasies means that you can direct your partner to what feels good for you. Authentic self-created sexual fantasies can enrich our sexual experiences and increase intimacy and pleasure. By contrast, sexual fantasies that are disturbing because they eroticize abusive or harmful aspects of a relationship are evidence of the meaner face of desire, wanting power over another.

When sex becomes entangled in power, you may come to believe that you are only an Object, that you function only to please your partner. This can quickly lead to sexual resentment and blame, but you may be denying that you have your own motives in wanting to confirm that you are beautiful or worthwhile through the desire in your partner's eyes.

Healthy sexual fantasies always include communication and trust, consent and equality, respect and mutual pleasure. Dialogue and negotiation are necessary ingredients in this kind of sexual partnership. Your partner may or may not choose to do what you want. You may or may not agree to your partner's desires, but you will respect them because they have been revealed with respect for you. Mature sexual partners talk about what they want and devise routines, practices, even roles to help them achieve pleasure in sex without offending or harming either partner. To begin a relationship of mature sexuality, both partners must relinquish the desire to have power over each other and embrace the desire for self-determination, sovereignty over their own desires.

Awakening Love between Equals

THE ANCIENT STORY of Psyche and Amor provides us with a rich account of the meaner face of female desire, brought into the light through loss of control. Although this story originally came from Greek mythology, its best-known version is Roman—from Ovid's *Metamorphoses* or *The Golden Ass*, a text written by Lucius Apuleius in the second century. My telling is loosely adapted from Apuleius through a contemporary translation. The subtleties of female desire alluded to in this story have been explored by many feminist writers, including Carol Gilligan and Florence Wiedemann and myself.

PSYCHE AND AMOR

Once upon a time, a king and a queen had three beautiful daughters. Much the most beautiful was Psyche, the youngest. People came from many lands just to witness the beauty of this young woman, some saying that she was Venus, the goddess of love, and others claiming that Psyche had replaced Venus as love's great goddess. Naturally, Venus was enraged by all the attention that Psyche—a mere mortal woman—had drawn away from her, so she poisoned the hearts of Psyche's suitors, leaving Psyche thoroughly rejected by men. Psyche's father, puzzled by the dearth of suitors for his beautiful daughter, began to suspect that something had gone awry with the gods.

In his search for an answer, the king consulted an oracle, through which Venus responded, telling him that his daughter was destined to marry a monster, a winged serpent that frightened even Jupiter (Zeus in Greek). She then instructed the king to have his daughter dressed in the clothes of mourning and to take her to a distant mountaintop where she would enter her death-marriage.

Psyche, accompanied by funeral music and her grieving parents, and dressed as a woman going to her grave, led her strange wedding procession to the mountaintop. At the summit her parents left her as they were instructed.

Alone in her dread, Psyche waited. Suddenly she was lifted by a gentle wind and carried over the side of the mountain until she landed in a fragrant, flowery field. A palace of gold and gems, filled with unbelievable beauty and treasures, rose before her. Thinking that perhaps she had died and this was the home of a god or goddess, Psyche entered and silently made her way from room to room. In a sumptuous bedroom invisible hands bathed and dressed her, and brought her all possible delicious foods and delightful comforts.

Adorned in the beautiful fabrics of the palace, comforted by the pleasures of her surroundings, Psyche fell into a deep sleep, only to be awakened at the stroke of midnight by a soft whisper. Knowing that anything might happen in this vast, uninhabited place, Psyche feared for her life and her chastity, but the whispering voice—a man's—reassured her: he would not force her or hurt her. Her invisible visitor embraced Psyche with unimaginable tenderness and made love to her in a most arousing and gentle way. Her own sexual desires were both stirred and satisfied in his embrace.

At the end of their night of passion, the visitor told her that he was her husband, but that she would never be allowed to see him. All her needs would be provided by invisible hands in the palace. As long as she did not try to find out who he was, they could continue to enjoy each other nightly.

At first Psyche willingly accepted these conditions. Amazed by the splendor and riches of her palace, she passed her days in pleasing occupations and spent her nights with her invisible husband. Shortly, though, Psyche began to miss her parents and her sisters. She longed to see them and to let them know that she had not died but was thriving in her new home. Psyche begged her husband to allow her to return to her family to reassure them of her safety and good fortune, and reluctantly he agreed. He instructed her to remember the conditions of their marriage: that she could neither know nor reveal his identity or all would come to an end.

Psyche returned to her family and proudly told them of her adventure—her journey over the mountainside, her glorious palace, and her gentle husband. Jealous of her good fortune, Psyche's sisters chided her and prattled about the dangers to which she had subjected herself. After all, they said, your husband may be a winged serpent, a monster of any kind, and you have surrendered yourself to him without knowing his real identity.

When Psyche returned to her palace, she had a plan that she and her sisters had devised to discover her husband's true nature. She prepared to encounter her husband armed with a knife and a candle. After they made love and while he slept, she lit the candle and raised it over his body. Before her was revealed the god Amor—the son of Venus—in all his beauty. Astonished by his glory, Psyche lurched back and dropped hot wax from her candle on his naked chest. Startled awake, Amor cursed her and fled. From atop a cypress tree he reproached his wife for her thoughtlessness and soared into the air. His identity revealed to a mortal, he had to return to his mother, never again to mingle with a mortal being.

Psyche's remorse was deep, and she wandered the earth in search of her beloved husband. Weary and hopeless, she came to a temple of Venus and entered, entreating the great goddess to help in this matter of love. Even more enraged at Psyche's alliance with Amor, Venus set up tasks for her daughter-in-law. Choosing feats that could never be accomplished by a mortal, Venus promised that Psyche would be reunited with Amor if she carried them out successfully.

Filled with faith in her great love for Amor, Psyche began her heroic adventure. Each step of the way powers of the natural world came to support both her courage and her love. Her final, most difficult task was to bring back a box of "beauty" from Proserpine (Persephone in Greek) of the underworld so that the aging Venus could restore her own appearance—faded from nursing her ailing son.

Helped by a talking stone tower, Psyche was given instructions on the exact steps to enter into, and be released from, the underworld. Returning with her final task fulfilled, Psyche foolishly decided to take advantage of some of Proserpine's beauty for herself. But Proserpine had placed death—not beauty—in the box to be taken to Venus. Upon opening the box, Psyche fell into a fatal sleep.

When he discovered his wife's fate, Amor begged his mother to allow Psyche to be made into an immortal goddess. In the end Venus conceded to her son's wishes. Amor rescued his wife from her death-sleep and brought her to heaven to be his timeless partner.

The Curse of Venus

THERE ARE MANY WAYS to interpret this complex story, but I will focus on the themes of sex through the looking glass— the seduction of power, competition among women, the split between pleasure and power in female sexuality, and the death of female sexual desire. By understanding this ancient tale as a story about the challenge to self-determination in female sexual desire, we come to see the sacrifice involved in being the desire-awakening maiden.

At the beginning of the story, Venus is the aging muse who fears being outdone by the beautiful young maiden. Venus knows the underlying reality of female power, that mortal women are extremely limited by male dominance. Psyche's only real power among humans is to attract a powerful man. Venus spoils this by eliminating men's desires to marry Psyche. We could interpret the curse of Venus as Psyche's muse complex, an obsession about her appearance that turns her beauty upside down and makes it into a liability. So Psyche becomes vulnerable to a death-marriage—a symbol of a total loss of power through marriage.

I have found many examples of the death-marriage theme in the dreams of women about to be married. One woman dreamt she willingly entered a grave or underground tunnel from which there was no escape. Another was present at her own funeral, dressed in her bridal gown. Marriage is, in a fundamental way, a psychological death of an old identity (as a single individual) and the beginning of a new identity (as a coupled individual). And for women there is an additional death: the adventure of being a bride comes to an end. Women are idealized as brides, not as wives. Some women fear the shift from muse to hag; they fear the weight of an unwanted identity laid upon them during or soon after the honeymoon. Many things previously attractive in a woman—her ambition, perseverance, intelligence—may be perceived as unattractive or even threatening after marriage.

Psyche is saved from her fear and humiliation by Amor. Who is Amor? Historically and mythically he is Eros (Cupid is his trivial name)—the image of love fulfilled. Amor is also the image of desire, born of pleasure's memory, in whose presence we long for more. When desire is blind or hidden, it becomes craving or impulse. Because it is the nature of desire to be felt as a lack, a memory, or a gap, we can be driven to fill its emptiness without knowing why.

Amor initially saves Psyche from the curse of Venus but blinds her to the knowledge of her own desire. Caught in a web of pleasures, Psyche is filled with desires and longing but has no self-determination or understanding of her circumstances. Becoming acquainted with her husband is forbidden. Even the hands that serve her are invisible. Recall my client Linda, who was caught in a cycle of dead-end relationships because, like Psyche, she was only her lover's Object of Desire. Blaming fate or her lovers, Linda knew nothing of her own desires, so she was deadened in her responses. Psyche's longing to return home is a longing to understand her own desire, to put together her past and her present.

But what Psyche finds at home is the divisiveness and spite of her jealous sisters. Like teenage girls directing their anger against a popular rival, Psyche's sisters attack her for being pampered and passive. As we saw in the double bind of female beauty, in place of female solidarity women join with men in reducing women to their appearances and divide themselves through competition, jealousy, and envy.

But sometimes the power mongering of others can awaken us to our hidden motives, and the competitive strivings of her sisters eventually lead Psyche to lift the candle and come to know her own desires. Yet Psyche carries out the action with candle and knife in hand because she is urged by her jealous sisters; she is not fully in possession of herself and acts carelessly in dropping the hot wax. Symbolically, Psyche's impulsive confrontation of Amor's identity reveals her still-developing sense of self-determination and desire to know about her own life and power.

The light of Psyche's candle reveals that Amor is a god. He is outside or beyond the human realm. With this knowledge Psyche loses Amor, not to be reunited with him until they become equals, when Psyche is immortal.

Like Amor, our sexual desires often escape us when we hastily cast the light of reality on arrangements that are hidden, unequal, without mutual consent and mutual pleasure.

If we are motivated primarily by wanting to be wanted, to reveal this hidden desire will chase away romantic feelings, but to keep it hidden entirely will rob us of our pleasures. Only when we know what motivates us are we free to choose alternatives.

Psyche is deeply grieved by the loss of Amor, but she cannot begin her transformation until she consults with Venus. In the myth Venus is a source of ancient knowledge about love, but we can also understand her as an aspect of Psyche's own complex, the source of some kind of ambivalence about herself. Venus assigns tasks to Psyche. Each one is a challenge to Psyche's ability to organize and take initiative, which are required lessons in becoming a Subject. The first tasks engage her in adventure, discernment, and courage. Creatures of nature (animals, plants, water) assist her in carrying out these feats. We can imagine this to mean that Psyche comes to understand her own nature—her instincts and intuitions.

Psyche's final task is the most difficult and important: she must enter the underworld, where mortals are forbidden to go. We can think of this as the realm of Psyche's unconscious fantasies and desires—the underworld of her sexual and other unknown longings. Venus has specifically set Psyche the task of stealing the ageless beauty of a goddess preserved in youth. Bringing this beauty back to Venus, Psyche is tempted to have some for herself and allows her impulse to rule her actions, recalling Pandora's impulsive curiosity in opening the earthenware jar.

At the moment she opens the box, Psyche becomes a Subject of her own desire. This is her first action not commanded by others. Although Psyche has developed some knowledge of her own nature and her ability to be competent and successful, she has continued to retain the hidden desire to be the most beautiful Object of Desire. Psyche is the potentially liberated woman who, like Princess Diana, still believes that power must be seduced rather than self-directed. Instead of completing the process of her autonomous development and earning the right to be Amor's equal, Psyche is annihilated by her hidden wish to retain the greatest beauty for herself. Once again she is at the mercy of fate as she falls into a death-sleep. This death-sleep is a parallel to her death-marriage at the start of the tale, a state of depression based on an impossible desire to be the ageless, desire-awakening maiden.

Her condition is reversed through the aid of Amor and Venus. Psyche is rescued by powers greater than herself, on whom she now depends. But she has learned the Subject lessons of self-determination well enough to become the equal of Amor. Psyche dies two deaths in the tale: the first as an unconscious Object of Desire and the second as a conscious Object of Desire, the muse who wants to be the ageless maiden. In dying the second death, Psyche is finally awakened on a higher level, an immortal herself and the Subject of her own desire.

The Dilemma of Sexual Self-Determination in Women

LEARNING HOW to be Subjects of their own sexual desires is both a confusing and complicated task for women in a world that is ruled by male sexual arousal and desire. Unable to awaken their own sexual pleasures and capacities, many women complain of feeling devitalized and even erotically dead. Wildly sexually active younger women and almost inactive midlife women have all told me about feeling confused, dissatisfied, restless, even bored by their sexual encounters.

Rarely—personally, socially, therapeutically—do I hear reports of ongoing sexual fulfillment in women. More often than not I hear about women wanting to be released from the "burden" of having to deal with men's sexual desires.

Midlife women in particular frequently tell me in therapy about how they experience more arousal and eroticism in conversations, movies, nursing their babies, masturbating, and fantasies than in having sexual encounters with their partners. These women tend to believe that they are having sex for their partners rather than themselves.

Marla and Jack, a couple in their early thirties with two preschool children, come to psychotherapy because their sex life has no vitality, almost no spark at all. Marla says that she doesn't desire sex anymore. She reports that she is willing to make love under some circumstances, and that she often enjoys it when she has it, but she isn't motivated to seek it. She believes that her lack of desire is connected to her husband's lack of intimacy. She says, "Jack treats me like an object."

Angry about this, she has decided that she will never again pretend to want sex when she doesn't feel the desire. From her perspective she has become sexually "liberated," claiming control over her own body. Marla is clear about wanting to keep this control until she is guaranteed an outcome different from what she has known: having sex primarily for Jack, gratifying his desires because she fears his agitation and anger when they don't have regular sex.

Jack sees things differently. He says he feels rejected by his wife. Since he believed he could become uncontrollably angry if he appealed to Marla directly for intimate sexual contact and she flatly refused, he agreed that she could have the sexual lead. But since the time they made this agreement, Marla has never pursued him sexually. Jack has consciously chosen to be somewhat emotionally distant from Marla to protect himself from his feelings of vulnerability and rejection. He isn't happy with this arrangement, but it is all he can do with his confusion and pain about the fact that Marla doesn't want him physically.

In our therapy sessions it became clear that Marla learned how to feel sexual only by looking sexy. In her adolescent and young adult years, she saw herself as "potentially attractive," by which she meant that she believed she looked "better than average" when she had on the right makeup and clothes. If a man lit up with excitement in her presence, this brought her pleasure and often left her feeling sexually aroused. But now Marla feels she is less desirable. She believes that her thighs are too heavy, and she doesn't like the thin wrinkle lines gathering around her mouth. Marla thinks that she couldn't attract a man again.

When she was young Marla learned how to flirt and charm, but she never learned how to have reliable sexual pleasure. Instead of having and practicing orgasm, she thought about and practiced being exciting and pretty. In those days she never felt that sexual arousal was in any way under her control. It just happened sometimes when she looked good and felt good about herself.

Without clear sexual needs of her own, Marla felt that she was having sex not for herself but rather because someone else wanted it. Even after she married Jack—who clearly desired her sexually—she never fully enjoyed intercourse, although she found the flirting, cuddling, and foreplay pleasant. Marla tried to have orgasms with Jack through manual stimulation, but she was too self-conscious. "It took too long; his arm almost fell off the last time we tried it." Although she could achieve orgasm alone, Marla eventually concluded that her body was just not as responsive as some women's. She initially thought she could have sex for Jack because he was unhappy without it. Then, a few months ago, she told Jack that she didn't want him to put any more pressure on her for sex, that she would ask for it when she wanted it. But she almost never wants it. Unconscious of her drive to be desired, she believes that her husband's emotional distance is most of the reason she doesn't want sex, yet she admits that she never really liked sex that much anyway. For her sex often wasn't pleasurable; sometimes it wasn't even pleasant.

By contrast, since adolescence Jack has known what gives him sexual pleasure, and he doesn't believe that Marla—an intelligent and perceptive person—could be so vague about and uninvolved with her own sexual desire. When asked directly whether he finds Marla attractive, Jack says, "Oh, sure," in a warm, convincing way. Both acknowledge that Jack's attraction to her is *not* the problem. He fears that Marla's lack of desire is his fault: maybe *he* doesn't have the right approach, the right body, or the right personality. He views her lack of sexual desire as a personal affront, and he becomes caught in wanting to be the Object of her desire.

But Jack's fears that the problem rests with him are mostly unfounded. At the root of their sexual difficulties is Marla's compulsion to be seen and reflected as sexy, arousing, beautiful. She learned to feel aroused when someone wanted her but not to develop her own sexual interest and pleasure. Now that she wants greater control over her life, Marla doesn't want to have sex *for* someone else. And Jack now shares in her predicament of wanting to be sexually desired himself. Neither partner seems able to budge in this sexual standstill; it's as though someone has turned off the key to their self-determination.

Following Psyche's lead, Marla must look into the darkness of her death-marriage and discover what her Amor looks like. Her desire has been for ageless beauty and the seduction of power, not for a sexual relationship that is mutually pleasurable. Marla's refusal to have sex "for" Jack could be seen as a first step toward admitting the truth of inner deadness, yet if she were to believe that exercising this kind of negative control is in fact freedom, she would never come to know herself as the Subject of her sexual desires. She has become a version of the hag in the woods—ashamed of her body, fighting feelings of inadequacy, afraid she is less female than other women, but determined to stick to her own experience in evaluating what she wants to do.

Like Psyche, Marla has been trapped in the dark. While she has learned how to excite others through touch and appearance, she is caught in someone else's (Jack's or the culture's) fantasy of the desire-awakening maiden. Afraid and angry, she has tried to call a halt to the pantomime, but doing so has also halted her own sexual development. She must allow her identity as a desire-awakening maiden to die in favor of a new identity, not as a hag but as a passionate partner, a loving friend, and a self-determining lover.

Through acknowledging her insecurities and sorting out how they are related to her hag and muse complexes, Marla can allow her old patriarchal identity to die. Like Psyche she has to practice courage and discernment to understand the meaner dynamics between her and other women, between her and Jack. For instance, Marla needs to acknowledge that she is obsessive about her appearance and constantly compares herself with younger, slimmer women. She needs to acknowledge her self-consciousness in the bedroom and learn how to relax, so that she can experience sexual pleasure instead of anxiety about her attractiveness. Rather than look to Jack to provide her with feelings of sexual worth, she must begin to explore her own wants. Only by acknowledging these aspects of the meaner face of her desires can Marla gradually free herself— body and mind—so that she can develop an atmosphere of eros and dialogue. Then she and Jack can talk respectfully about their pleasures and needs.

True Love

NATURALLY THIS KIND of conversation includes a greater vulnerability and openness, a willingness to be authentic in the presence of a partner. As I talked about it in the first chapter, authenticity opens the possibility for real love. Many people tell me that they don't really know what "love" is and that they believe the word is overused. *Love* means a particular kind of connection, and it cannot be overused or overspoken.

As the poet Octavio Paz described it, true love can happen only when desire meets reality. Until Psyche could see Amor, she shaped his image through her projections and fears. Although she desired Amor, she could not love him because she did not know him. When he was revealed she lost him— symbolizing the loss of the romantic ideal in favor of the real, authentic knowledge of a partner. Amor fled because he was not human but idealized as a god. Psyche could return to him in the end because she had become his equal, and she had accomplished the tasks of courage and discernment that allowed her to become a Subject of Desire.

Love—one of the most transcendent of human feelings— emerges only after you and your beloved are deeply known to each other. Knowing and tolerating your own and your partner's vulnerabilities, frailties, needs, and limitations allows you to gradually recognize that you cannot bring another under your control through seduction or desire. The other will be who he or she is. A deep and abiding affection for someone you know and accept, someone you realize is not under your control, is love. Love—including erotic love—teaches us that though we have limitless desires, we have limited control, and paradoxically the only way to transcend our limitations is to love others in their imperfection.

Freeing Ourselves from Male Fantasies

THE DILEMMA OF female sexual desire is that the light of truth turned on our desires will reveal that we live in a world of male sexual imagination. What has been hidden from our awareness is the anxiety, contempt, *and* desire we feel in relation to male images of erotic female power. These are the products of our often hidden power plays in response to male fantasies that continue to hold sway over the collective imagination. We may be tempted to believe that sexual desire is primarily male, and that withholding compliance is our only freedom, but ultimately this mistaken belief cuts us off from our own erotic imaginations, the possibility of discovering and acting on our authentic pleasures and needs.

Only when we take full responsibility for how we have knowingly or unknowingly played out the power dynamics of the male imagination—in wanting to be or envying the Object of Desire—can we learn to connect freely to ourselves and others without excessive self-consciousness and control. This freedom is the product of knowledge, especially self-knowledge. To be accountable for your own desires, both the meaner and the kinder ones, is to take the first step toward being able to act as a whole person, as someone who can tolerate and accept a variety of motives in yourself and others.

In itself the desire to be seen as attractive or powerful is not negative. Indeed it probably arises from wanting to know that one's love is good. Even as infants we want to give our affection to others, not simply receive from them. The give-and-take of love, one of the earliest dialogues in human life, depends on being loved *and* lovable. Wanting to be wanted can be healthy and engaging when it is playful and light, and remains in the service of love.

Then it does not become a deadening compulsion that overtakes our erotic pleasures and desires. As the story of Psyche shows us, we can free ourselves from our hidden desires by bringing them into the light, then we can develop ourselves as erotic partners by claiming our equality and freedom. As erotic partners in fully passionate embraces, we can learn to transcend our ordinary boundaries of self-other through the practice of sexual love. We women have this possibility within our grasp when we can dissolve the self-hatreds and self-consciousness that keep us unknowingly focused on power rather than love.

FOUR

Hothouse Mothering
and the Divine Child

THERE IS MUCH about contemporary motherhood that keeps mothers unknowingly focused on hidden needs for power, on wanting to be wanted. Idealizing motherhood—speaking only of wonder, nurturance, and goodness in the mother-child relationship—encourages us to believe that Mother is the most critical ingredient in child development, and that mothering is the most important task a woman can perform.

As in the 1950s and '60s, many Americans today seem to believe that conscientious mothering contributes more to our future than any other work a woman can do. Midlife and younger women contemplate the decision of whether to become a mother with awe and uncertainty, but they are influenced by friends and media to believe that a full-time emotional commitment to mothering—especially for infants and young toddlers—is the *most* important role a woman can assume.

This basic assumption about the singular importance of Mother—exclusive of Father, peers, the broader cultural context—is highly misleading and often wrong. Many influences that shape a child's life, from the norms and values of our society to a child's peers, can be more important to identity formation and lifelong development. Certainly the father and other adults can be as important as caregivers and role models as the mother is, and individual temperament, sibling order, developmental potentials, and unpreventable circumstances all play major roles in determining who a child will become.

The image of the perfect mother (selfless, tireless, generous, inventive, a good cook) is the bane of every mother's existence. Wanting to be wanted, mothers often strive to fulfill this wounding ideal of perfect selflessness. Cut off from their own desires and pleasures, unaware of how much they want to be admired, mothers can become anxious, depressed, even dissociated from themselves, filled with worry and fear about the details of their children's behaviors and surroundings.

"Hothouse mothering" is promoted by this mixture of idealization and anxiety: a complete absorption in the child's or children's world, leading to an all-consuming identification with the mother role, with how well the child is developing, and with how close to "perfection" the mother-child connection is.

Women cannot be faulted for wanting to be perfect mothers; once again they appear to be offered power in a society that repeatedly declares a mother's irreplaceable importance. Yet they never see this power materialize, and they are never invited to explore their feelings of betrayal and anger at the ways they are disappointed and exploited by society and by their offspring. Many mothers of grown-up children talk regretfully about having spent the better part of their adult years "sacrificing" for their children, who, now fully grown, are often critical of their mother. We give only lip service to the idea that mothers are to be honored and loved; children do not feel responsible for sustaining an interest in their mothers' lives. Mother is perceived simply as a *resource* for others' needs rather than as a person in her own right, and many mothers lose themselves in the role.

The anxiety and idealization of hothouse mothering are not the invention of women but the product of our collective inability to respond to the physical and psychological needs of parents of young children, especially mothers. There are no choices available in many areas of responsibility for the developing child. All too often Mother is the only person whom teachers, relatives, neighbors hold accountable for the child's welfare and protection. Without an outlet for expressing their anger at being exploited and manipulated through idealization—isn't it just *wonderful* being a mother!—mothers unconsciously turn resentment and fear into shame and guilt about themselves. Women who struggle every day to do the best possible job as mothers feel constantly inferior to the task, afraid that their shortcomings are the primary reason they cannot measure up to the image of the ideal mother.

Of Woman Born

I AM A MOTHER myself—to my two biological children and to four stepchildren. In mothering these six young people, I was challenged and grew and changed. I love them all and have encountered each one in both exhilarating and exhausting ways, but most of all I came to admire and respect them for the strong, compassionate people they are. In their twenties and thirties now, they have all graduated from college and are useful citizens. They are their own people, as indeed they have always seemed to me to be.

I view myself as a successful mother who has been deeply engaged in being a parent but also deeply engaged with other things. My relationships with my grown-up children are fun, demanding, fascinating, and complex. I still become unduly involved in their vulnerabilities and life stresses, and I have had my share of anxiety, fear, shame, and guilt. But however much I have doubted my own mothering habits, practices, and methods along the way of their growing up, I never doubted that I loved my children and wished them well. I am no different from most mothers in this way.

I became a mother when many of my peers were heading into careers. Married to an older man and uncertain about my future, I got pregnant in my twenties—during the early 1970s—when feminism was just beginning to sway American women away from the traditional roles of wife and mother.

My unexpected ambivalence about being a parent to my first biological child, and my haunting, irrational fears of doing harm to her, roiled inside me after only a few weeks of single-handed responsibility for my infant daughter. I could find nothing in the child-rearing manuals at my disposal, nothing in the faces or voices of my cousins who were also young mothers, and no hint in my mother's face to indicate that my ambivalent feelings (especially the fleeting impulse to suffocate my infant) were normal or even imaginable. So I hid my feelings and read everything about motherhood I could find in

psychoanalytic and feminist literature, only to be further mad-
dened by what I encountered there: either mothers were
blamed for all their children's problems (psychoanalysis) or
they were analyzed in vaguely Marxist terms (feminism), but
their experiences and development were not recorded. I felt
sure that I was potentially psychotic in some way that would
manifest itself during a difficult middle-of-the-night feeding.
And then I found Adrienne Rich's *Of Woman Born*, in which
she seemed to address me directly in her historical and personal account of being a mother. Words like these became my
lifeline:

> That calm, sure, unambivalent woman who moved
> through the pages of the [infant care] manuals I read
> seemed as unlike me as an astronaut. . . . Throughout
> pregnancy and nursing, women are urged to relax, to
> mime the serenity of madonnas. No one mentions the
> psychic crisis of bearing a first child, the excitation of
> long-buried feelings about one's own mother, the sense
> of confused power and powerlessness, of being taken
> over on the one hand and of touching new physical and
> psychic potentialities on the other. . . . No one men-
> tions the strangeness of attraction—which can be as
> single-minded and overwhelming as the early days of a
> love affair—to a being so tiny, so dependent, so folded-
> in to itself—who is, and yet is not, part of oneself.

Rich's reflections and knowledge liberated me. Reading and
rereading her account of her own maternal being was the
only thing that sustained me in the first year of my daughter's life.

Now I feel almost lucky that I became a mother so young and so set apart from my peers. I had only my cousins, living hundreds of miles away, and the strangers on the street and in the pediatrician's office to advise me. Early on I recognized that being a mother evokes a lot of advice from others, mostly unasked for and often unwelcome. Both women and men would speak to me in the most personal terms on the streets, in shopping malls, in women's rest rooms—advising me on nursing, disciplining my daughter, telling me how to feed and clothe her. Suddenly I was the center of attention, but in a way that was destabilizing and often deeply confusing. I heard a lot about others' experiences and was never asked about my own. I heard many idealizing comments (How wonderful! How beautiful! How special!) but almost nothing about the confusion that haunted me. But because the people advising me were largely strangers, I could set their advice aside and return to Rich's wisdom, settle into my own experience, keep a journal, and determine to free myself from cultural prejudices.

I made friends with other mothers who had children the same age as my daughter, but I did not put much stock in their warnings and admonitions either. Many of them were doing what their mothers did, but I knew that I didn't want the life my mother had had. Most of my close friends were not having babies, nor did they even seem to be interested in the fact that I had. They were focused on going to graduate school, figuring our their own lives, finding a love affair that might last. They seemed to trust that I was a good-enough mother in a general way, and that soothed me.

The media had lost sight of motherhood for a few years there in the seventies, because feminism and the counterculture were drawing attention away from the more traditional themes of family. Looking back, I recognize how I was able to find my own way into my experiences, and to feel the guilt and anxiety of my complexes as *my* complexes and not as some reality that meant I was not an adequate mother.

A friend of my husband once said that she had had her babies when her "hormones were high and brainpower low," and I feel something similar. I didn't give a lot of thought to having children; I wanted them and I had them. Frequently I reminded myself that all adults had arrived here the same way—through mothers. Therefore, I would think, I can be okay with this; no matter how badly I feel I'm doing, I'll muddle through as well as most. And I know now that I wasn't doing badly in my relationship with my daughter or in my care for her; it was only in my feelings that I suffered. I was afraid of the range of negative, primitive feelings coupled with swollen, prideful ones. I was both enraptured with this baby and angry that she had stolen my life from me.

It is significant that I became a feminist at just about the same time I became a mother. Rich's book taught me my first feminist lesson: that my experience as a woman was not in the cultural record, and that I should not measure myself against that record, especially in regard to motherhood. I quickly saw that I needed to hold a strong distinction between the *ideal* of motherhood and my experiences as a mother.

That deep insight has served me well. By the end of the first year of my daughter's life, I was in psychotherapy, exploring how to put together my life in terms of the specifics of things meaningful to me, as a woman and an equal partner and parent. Daring, sustaining, challenging, and purposeful, my life would encompass a context bigger than wife and mother yet integrate these roles into it, I said to myself. I wanted to make creative use of the awesome responsibility, tender moments, and tearful mistakes that are the stuff of mothering; I wanted to read and write about it, to teach it, and to help women recognize and understand the ambivalence of it.

From the constraints of my mother's life—as a working-class wife and stay-at-home mother—I concluded that I did not want to be a full-time mother, without other work that I could love. Besides, I needed to work for a living because my husband and I could not support our family on his income alone. I knew also that I didn't want to be a full-time professional without children, because I loved a home that was filled with life. And my home was soon that—filled with children and stepchildren and pets and plants and lots of energy.

When my children were toddlers, I went back to graduate school and became a psychologist, then moved from the Midwest to teach in a women's college on the East Coast. While teaching developmental psychology to graduate students, I searched for a book that would situate the experience of being a mother in a bigger context than attachment theory and children's development. I wanted my students to understand mothering as distinct from motherhood and to penetrate the social commentary that makes motherhood seem so ideal and pressures mothers to want to be perfect.

Hothouse Mothering

I FOUND A revolutionary book, *Inventing Motherhood*, by Ann Dally, an English psychiatrist, that put into context a mother's dilemma of anxiety and betrayal. In relating the special difficulties of women in my mother's generation—those who gave birth in the decade after World War II—Dally

describes what I am calling hothouse mothering: the preoccupied style of mothering that inflates a mother's every decision
with portents of future meaning.

This style of mothering is both relatively new and scientifically indefensible. As Dally points out, few of us have a historical perspective on child rearing or any suspicion that what we
may consider most "natural" for mothers and children—leaving mothers alone with their children—had never been tried
before the mid–twentieth century. Instead, we claim to have a
"scientific" account, in which we supposedly understand what
is best for a child's development.

Yet it is odd, as she points out, how so-called scientific theories of child development that focus almost exclusively on the
mother-child pair have paralleled the idealization of motherhood and the ways in which women have been promoted as
ideal nurturers of their children. As Dally says,

> When large numbers of mothers have never before the
> mid–twentieth century been shut up alone with their
> small children for most of their working hours, suddenly
> it appeared that this was the ideal, the norm, essential for
> the healthy psychological development of the child and
> a demonstration of feminine normality in the mother.

Looking at how today's adults—reared in the first era of hothouse mothering—appear to compare with adults of the past,
Dally suggests that we might conclude that "the era of unbroken and exclusive maternal care has produced the most neu-
rotic, disjointed, alienated and drug-addicted generation ever
known."

Many of us in the baby boomer generation grew up in the
exclusive company of one adult at home: a depressed mother

who was frustrated by her isolation and unaware of her frustration. No doubt it is better to grow up with at least one adult in charge than with no adults at all, but the hothouse isolation of women and children has produced psychological difficulties that are rarely expressed in any media accounts of mothers, working mothers, attachment bonds, or child development. In my practice of psychotherapy, I mostly treat the effects of negative mother complexes: the ways that now-grown-up children internalized the expectations and anxieties of a woman with whom they often felt emotionally trapped.

Even the most nurturant mother, when she is alone with her children for too long, will have episodes of depression, anxiety, or agitation that can feel dangerous to a dependent child. When mothers are left unsupported and have no choices about where they can direct their attention, they are even more likely to become immersed in self-conscious emotions (shame, envy, guilt, pride, jealousy) that interfere with their ability to concentrate directly on their activities. In comparing themselves (sometimes obsessively) with the ideals of motherhood, women increase their feelings of inferiority and self-consciousness and long to be wanted, admired, validated. And, of course, they turn to their children for these things.

Liz is an example of a contemporary hothouse mother. She came to psychotherapy because her husband, Frank, recommended it. He was afraid of her intense emotional needs and ruminations, with which she confronted him when he returned from work at the end of a long day of physical and emotional demands.

Liz is in her late twenties. She had been a successful insurance adjuster before she began to stay at home as a full-time mother with her first child, Julie, who was one year old when Liz began therapy. "At first I thought that my angry, scared feelings were related to not wanting to get pregnant again. Frank and I have always talked about having a second child close to the first. Lately I have been panicked at the thought." Liz explained that she had just begun to feel that she had her body back to normal. She had stopped nursing and was now within five pounds of her prepregnancy weight. "And I just started to take some dance classes on Tuesday nights. I don't want to give those up."

Liz feels good about how Julie is doing. "I can tell that Julie is a happy, normal baby—and sometimes when she laughs at me or makes one of her funny faces, I think I'll just explode with pride and joy. But then I realize that Julie can't be the only person who makes me feel good. In fact, that's probably a big problem. I don't really feel very good about myself or Frank these days."

Liz said she thought that Frank was angry because together they had initially decided that she would leave her work, be a full-time mom, and have their two children close together. "Now that I'm not ready, I think he's frustrated. Not only that, when he asked me recently when I *would* be ready, I told him maybe *never*. I don't know if I want to have another child." When we talked about why Liz had changed her mind, she said, "Becoming a mother has changed me. I used to be a friend, a professional, a wife. Now I'm just a mom twenty-four hours a day. Although I love Julie, and being Julie's mom, I feel like other parts of myself are dying. That scares me, and Frank doesn't understand at all."

From her description of her daily life, it was clear how isolated Liz had become, especially from her professional friends. She often felt incapable of making a phone call or having lunch with an old friend she didn't seem to have anything in common with anymore. At home with Julie, she could go through an entire day without speaking to another adult. "When Frank walks through the door, he's never sure if he's going to speak to a sane adult or some screaming banshee. I can talk his ear off or give him the cold shoulder without a moment's notice. I'm really angry that he still has his old life and I don't. And, of course, I *know* it's not fair to be angry with him. After all, I chose to stay at home with Julie."

Frank and Liz rarely relate as a couple anymore. Finances are tight now that they don't have Liz's income, and she feels guilty about paying a baby-sitter so that they can go out alone together. Frank is working extra hours, and he usually doesn't get home until 8:00 P.M., when Liz is exhausted. They fall into bed at 10:00, and Liz then finds herself feeling angry that she is so tired. "I'm so tired of being needed by Julie. There's nothing left to give to Frank, and I honestly tend to blame *him* for the situation I am in, although I know that's irrational."

Yet, like many hothouse mothers, Liz is quick to defend her choice. "I have always felt that I would be the best caregiver for my child. Who else could be more interested in her? Why should I have strangers raising her if I can afford to do it myself?" When Liz thinks back to her own childhood, she says she wants to be a "more involved mother than my mother was. I was a 'latchkey' kid after my mom and dad divorced and my mom went out to work as a secretary. I always felt responsible for my younger brother, and he was usually mad at me for bossing him around. I want to do a better job than my mom did."

Liz's mother lives in a nearby town, and she is very supportive of Liz staying at home full-time with Julie. "My mom says now that she feels really guilty for the problems that my brother has. He didn't do very well in high school and got mixed up in drugs. She wants me to do a better job than she did, and she's always willing to take care of Julie, but my mom's still working, and she doesn't have much time, except on weekends."

Liz believes that she is lucky to have a choice. She seems unaware that her "choice" is embedded in a social and cultural context of what is ideal for a child: care from a full-time mother at home. She assumes that her decision is best for Julie, even though Liz has never examined the long-term losses (such as a more harmonious relationship with Frank) to both herself and Julie that her decision implies.

Liz unknowingly increases the guilt her own mother feels about her brother by failing to assign it where it rightfully belongs—to Liz's father, the school system, and a lot of other people who failed to lend a hand in assisting her mother in raising healthy children. Taking on all the responsibility for Julie's development and welfare seemed to Liz to be normal, natural. "Everyone agreed. But there are days when I'm just miserable and feel that the 'choice' to be a full-time mom doesn't seem to be mine. Why did everyone, including me, seem to assume that I'd be the best parent, the one to stay at home? And why didn't anyone tell me that it would be so hard?"

The Invention of Motherhood

THERE HAVE ALWAYS been mothers, but motherhood (like childhood) was only recently invented. Not until the Victorian era did motherhood first emerge in popular literature as a social concept. Earlier it was just a fact: one was a mother or not. But in the later part of the nineteenth century, being a mother became associated with the virtues of nurturance and femininity, and phrases such as "true motherhood" were used to describe an ideal condition imposed on women's mothering.

Victorian mothers were often depicted in paintings or early photos as angelic, madonnalike, and serene. One can't imagine that these mothers ever directed a cross word at their children. Perhaps they never did; they were not full-time mothers. As Dally points out, the mothers pictured in these idealized portraits were privileged women who did not provide direct care for their children but had wet nurses at birth and nannies later. The aesthetic and cultural origin of idealized motherhood is the privileged mother who saw her children only when they were bathed and fed, and could be enjoyed. When contemporary full-time mothers are urged to see themselves as versions of the idealized mother, ironically they lack the information that the unambivalent, smiling madonna had a lot of hired help.

In the past, middle- and upper-class women hired servants to care for their children, while farming and working women relied on aunts and grannies; children and mothers were rarely alone and isolated. Before mothers were meant to be the singular caregivers for their children, they were portrayed as gentler and kinder than mother substitutes. The latter were regularly depicted in childhood stories and nursery rhymes as witchy images of the split-off hatred and resentment that develop in children because of their long dependence and powerlessness.

Recall the mean nanny, the nasty older sister, the crabby maiden aunt, and the dreaded stepmother of folk and fairy tales. These archetypal figures of the hag-bitch are blamed for destroying the child's fragile soul, while Mother is preserved as saintly. The fact was that these mother subs often did most of the disciplining, and, as we saw in the first chapter, it has always been easy to demonize a woman who expresses a power-ful negative emotion. No doubt there were caregivers—older siblings, poor house servants, and others—who were bitter and spiteful, jealous of the more pampered mama. No doubt they took out their resentments on the children, but I also believe that the mother subs were especially negativized because the dangerous hostility of a child's dependence could be safely pro-jected onto them, preserving the image of a good and wise mother.

Idealization can be understood as a feeling of love isolated from hate for someone whom you actually love and hate. The image of the idealized must be elevated in order to hide its shadow, its darker component. The hatred is kept out of aware-ness, and the love becomes unrealistic and fanciful. Fantasies of perfection prevent the hate from becoming conscious. If someone were to suggest that hate is present along with love, angry feelings would be provoked.

The idealized mother of the Victorian era could be admired for her constantly loving nature because she was often unavail-able. Perhaps she *was* more enthusiastic and positive when she engaged with her children than the full-time mother can often be. It is most important, though, to recognize that the unambivalently loving and nurturant mother—the origin of our ideals of motherhood—is not a full-time mother but some-one privileged enough to hire a nurse or nanny to carry out the more difficult and/or dirty tasks.

What we now expect of a full-time mother—a deeply felt connection with her infant, a desire for a better life for her child than for herself, and a devotion to the needs of each child—increases her fearful responsibility for her child's wel-fare. Consciously or unconsciously, a mother often fears her negative feelings and splits them off into attacks on her partner or herself so that her feelings will not endanger her child. In this situation, especially in the context of the idealization of motherhood, a woman will either come to see herself as the dreaded hag-bitch or believe that her partner, her own mother, or someone else is sucking her dry of vitality. Like Liz, most mothers attempt to protect their children from such negative feelings. If these split-off feelings are enacted against the child, a mother may become abusive—usually in an instant in which she suddenly feels enraged at her child. Alternatively, if the mother feels a flash of rage or hatred at the child but does not attack, she may believe that she is an abusive mother even though she has not really enacted her hostility.

Idealizing our children or our mothers suppresses our guilt and anxiety about our hateful feelings, but it prevents us from knowing the truth of the ambivalence involved in the long dependence of human children. Especially in a society like ours, which hypervalues independence, adolescent and some-times even adult children *are* free to express their hostility about dependency needs. Biting the hand that feeds them, they issue complaints, criticisms, even open attacks aimed at reducing the inner importance of Mother. This kind of adoles-cent hostility is portrayed in TV shows and movies, but rarely with any sympathy for the mother. More often the mother is the target of damning humor or criticism. Mothers themselves rarely get equal time, either at home or in the movies, to express their feelings about the long dependence of their chil-dren or their responses to being vilified by adolescent humor.

Instead of allowing mothers to become aware of the range of ambivalent feelings that are a part of mothering, the doctrine of hothouse mothering encourages us to become increasingly self-conscious about whether we are meeting the demands of the ideal. Are we adequately selfless, courageous, calm, assured, patient, nurturant? Hothouse mothering promotes total identification with the child's needs and wants, so much so that we become oblivious to the needs and wants of other adults around us as well as our own. We are dominated by wanting to be wanted by our child or children and wanting to be validated and seen as ideal mothers. Having no world outside such an obsession with motherhood, a woman can get lost in a hall of mirrors that distort her feelings of worth and her ability to see where she is useful and successful.

Having worthwhile work outside the home, and effective child care for dependent children, can be a step toward healthy mothering for a woman and her child or children. But a social climate of hothouse mothering spoils the ameliorative effects of mothers having lives of their own. It undermines social supports for effective child care from mother subs and encourages women to feel ashamed and guilty for wanting a life separate from child-rearing responsibilities. So-called expert advice has seemed to make it impossible for women to wholeheartedly practice the more traditional form of child rearing: having diverse activities in their lives and sharing mothering responsibilities with a variety of others.

Attachment Theory

As MOST PEOPLE KNOW, two-thirds of all American mothers of dependent children are now in the labor force. More mothers than nonmothers have paid jobs or are actively looking for them. Most working mothers have full-time jobs—thirty-five hours or more weekly. Yet in place of developing support systems that would help women combine work and family, we continue to extend and develop beliefs that full-time mothers are the best caregivers for their children. Naturally this has encouraged a bad case of hothouse mothering in women who stay home to care for children, and perhaps an even worse case of guilt and anxiety in the majority of women, who are employed away from home.

A great deal has been written about the "second shift" of work and responsibility faced by mothers when they arrive home from the workplace. In part this problem arises from the idealization of motherhood: fathers, relatives, and hired help aren't as ideal as the mother. In part it arises from the lack of power (status, income, decision making) connected to mothering itself and the reality of the universal ambivalence felt by children toward their caregivers. In part it arises from the fact that effective, safe child care is not available to many poor, working-class, and even middle-income mothers. Whether the mother works outside the home or not, the psychological condition of hothouse mothering—as it affects mothers and children—is neither natural nor healthy.

Much of what we currently regard as a scientific defense for the singular importance of the mother comes from attachment theory and a set of studies carried out on British children separated from their parents during and after World War II. Attachment theory is a model of different "patterns of attachment" that are formed in our earliest dependent relationships. Early bonding, characterized as secure, anxious, or avoidant, has been shown to carry over to later personal development through our abilities, self-confidence, and emotional tendencies in relationship.

Psychiatrists Rene Spitz and John Bowlby were the original authors of the studies investigating the attachment behaviors of war orphans. These first studies were used to draft an official

British governmental document that encouraged women to leave their places in the work world and become full-time caregivers for their children when their husbands returned from the war. The original studies, based on children who were left in dire circumstances without contact with their parents, do not readily generalize to the child who is left in effective child care.

Later attachment studies, though, especially through the pioneering work of Mary Main and her colleagues, did show that all children develop certain patterns of attachment in infancy that have important effects on other areas of their functioning, such as self-confidence, emotional security, and achievement. In my therapeutic practice and in my writings and teaching, I have made ample use of attachment theory and research findings. I am convinced that our early bonds do carry over into our later adult bonds and identity formation, although with mediating effects throughout childhood and adolescence. Mapping relational styles in terms of the three major attachment patterns—secure, anxious, and avoidant—*is* useful to psychotherapists for diagnosing and helping with problems in childhood and adult relationships.

However, it is misleading to use these findings to support the singular importance of a full-time mother. From attachment research we know that children normally form their original attachment bonds in the first six months of life. This is a fundamental base for later development. During these first six months, a normal infant can form attachment bonds with at least three or four, and probably up to five or six, caregivers who can function as this secure base. If this were not so, earlier generations would have been seriously impaired, because infants were often cared for by several people—an older sibling, a hired helper, a nanny, a grandmother, or a neighbor, in addition to the mother.

Until modern birth control a woman was pregnant an average of fifteen times during her adult life and so was giving birth or lactating most of the time. Older siblings and other helpers cared for the younger ones as much as the mother did. Also, mothers did not cherish each individual infant as a unique personality, as we now do. As Dally reminds us, "Two centuries ago, of every four babies born alive, only one was likely to be alive on its first birthday. . . . The death rate between the ages of one and five was a further eighteen per cent, and the death rate throughout the rest of youth was also very high." Although infant mortality has fallen steadily in the past two hundred years, it was still high during the early part of the twentieth century. Only since World War II have parents been able to be reasonably confident that their children would survive.

What was it like to be a mother with the possibility that at least half of your children would fail to survive long enough to grow into adolescents? Losing one's children through death was regarded as a natural part of life; thus it was important to have as many children as possible so that at least some might survive. Although grief over the loss of an infant or child is clearly universal, mothers of the past seem to have had a more resigned, even detached, attitude. For example, Dally quotes one devoted mother of many children in the 1770s, who writes in her journal after the death of a newborn: "One cannot grieve after her much, and I have just now other things to think of." Often two children in the same family were given the same first name so that at least one of them might carry the name into adulthood. Mothers were more emotionally reserved about their involvement because it wasn't clear that an individual child would survive until that child had reached some maturity, often adolescence.

In contrast, our current tendency to see each child as unique, and each mother as solely responsible to develop that unique potential, is a very recent development coming directly from official British and American decisions to proselytize women to leave the workplace to make room for men returning from World War II. John Bowlby was swept up into this movement not only because he was a psychoanalyst and scientist but because he was raised by a nanny.

A product of the British upper classes, Bowlby had seen his mother from a distance that permitted him to think she would be the most important person for his development. Of Bowlby, Dally writes,

> He feels that mothers should be there all the time, as he puts it "constant attention day and night, seven days a week and 365 in the year." This is to him much more important than how a mother feels about it, whether it suits her personality and ultimately her children, or what happens if she can't do it. . . . Children brought up by nannies tend to idealize their mothers. They see her from afar and think how wonderful it would be if they could be looked after by her.

Many current studies are as slanted as Bowlby's biases, assuming that the mother's constant presence is the ideal condition for the child. Most popular and scientific manuals and standards for mothering are based on studies of animals, tribal peoples, or working-class and lower-middle-class mothers. The scientists who do the studies and write the books investigate either captive groups or those who need money and can be paid to be studied. Studies of mothering are usually written without reference to the social contexts of participants, although the type of attention and care provided by caregivers—mothers and others—might be affected by social and financial conditions. The old system of paid help—nannies or other employed helpers—still exists among privileged people, but it is not widely studied because this group does not need the money paid by researchers.

Journalist Joan Peters's book, *When Mothers Work*, is an exception. In her interviews with working mothers who are able to find good hired help to care for their children, she discovered that both mothers and children benefit from the mothers' employment away from home. Drawing on a wide range of studies to back her findings, Peters also shows that good outside child care, even for infants under six months, puts children at no risk and sometimes gives a developmental advantage over full-time home care.

Yet the notion that a young child should have the constant and exclusive attention of a full-time mother (supplemented by times with the father on weekends and evenings) has replaced the more traditional situation of a mother sharing her children—right from birth—with grandmothers, aunts, nannies, fathers, older siblings, neighbors, workmates, and friends. In this current period of backlash against feminism, women have been once again convinced of the enormous importance of full-time mothering, especially for young children.

The Divine Child

PART AND PARCEL of our present idealization of the mother is idealization of the child. The healthy infant (equipped to be lovable and very dependent) draws an idealizing love from parents and others. Accompanying this normal tendency to see the infant as a most desirable creature is an emotional pull toward imagining an extraordinary potential contained in the infant. Carl Jung described this universal emotional pull as the "archetype of the Divine Child."

Archetype literally means "primary imprint," and it refers to a universal tendency for humans to form certain emotionally charged images. We humans are designed in such a way that we form internal images (based on our subjective experiences, not on fact) of those on whom we depend and those who endanger us, especially in our early years. Once we have formed an archetypal image (of a demanding Terrible Mother, for example), we unconsciously import it into our later development by imposing it on new situations. We cannot escape the emotional tendency to do this; even after we become conscious of the tendency, we still have it, although we can diminish its influence on our actions.

A psychological complex gradually evolves from myriad experiences in which we impose such an image on our perceptions and then respond emotionally in a certain way. These images— such as the Great and the Terrible Mother, the Divine Child, the Demon, and the Great Father—show up as symbols in religions, art, dreams, and other creative expressions among human beings everywhere. Each new stage of life brings some fresh potentials for new archetypal images (for example, images of illness and decay usually emerge only later in life), but we are always recycling the ones from our earliest years because they are so fundamentally compelling. Many of them were formed in our early attachment relationships and gave us a sense of being able to cope with the reality around us before we had any concept or use of language.

The Divine Child is an easily recognized archetypal image. This is an image of a child who is extraordinary, with enormous gifts and promise. In most world religions we find the symbol of the Divine Child—like the infant Siddhartha (later to become the Buddha), who can at his birth walk and speak about his profound spiritual nature. The baby Jesus is another example, recognized by wise men to hold greater potential than kings and poets.

The symbol of the Divine Child is an expression of that tremendous power of the infant to stir imagination and possibility, and to encourage us to believe in new beginnings. In dreams, for example, the extraordinary infant who walks and talks and performs feats most often symbolizes the potential for a new beginning in ourselves. And, of course, each infant *is* a new beginning.

But we all risk investing our babies with such potential that we consciously or unconsciously believe they will save us from the suffering and miseries of our ordinary lives. You have probably heard about or known parents who spend all their waking hours developing the musical, mathematical, theatrical, or athletic ability of an unusually gifted child. Rarely is this child happy and securely attached. Instead the child is co-opted into an arrangement whereby he or she is to provide the parents with a certain magic. Sustaining the supposed powers of the Divine Child, the parents provide the constant attention, day and night, that Bowlby asks of mothers. But that attention is bound to the parents' wishes for the child and is usually not in the best interest of the child. The child's attachment bonds are then marked by anxiety and resentment about having to please and fulfill the parents' dreams.

Sacrificed in the process is the development of the child's autonomy—that source of action and self-knowledge that permits us to become self-determining adults. The sense of autonomy, the conviction that our feelings and motivations are genuinely ours, is a precious human capacity that comes from a childhood in which there was both love and discipline from a variety of adults. As we have seen throughout, girls and women do not develop an easy autonomy because they are promised false powers for being desirable, nice, pretty, and popular instead of being clearly encouraged and rewarded for self-determination. But a child of either sex can surrender its autonomy in the face of parents' wishes and demands to be a Divine Child.

Many hothouse mothers believe that their child or children are extraordinary in some positive way. The idealization of mothers includes the belief that children, especially babies, are *wonderful*. Hothouse mothering is about the most *wonderful* child, who shows what a *wonderful* mother you are. As I said earlier, this situation prevents us from becoming conscious of the ambivalence of a normal parent-child bond.

The normal hatred that arises in a parent-child relationship is the reaction of both people to the long dependency period, in which a human being is readied for a responsible adulthood. During this time—anywhere from eighteen to twenty-five years in our society now—the child comes to feel infuriated and resentful of being so powerless and subordinate. As I mentioned earlier, adolescent children in America often openly express the hostility they feel about their dependency. A parent, especially a full-time mother, is apt to feel equally hostile about the needs, demands, and impulses of a child, but she suppresses this anger.

As all parents know, power struggles abound at each new stage of development in the child's life, and good parents learn how to guide the process of autonomy through discipline and punishment in the earlier years, and example and advice in the later ones. This is a demanding, strategic job—neither fun nor wonderful and full of potential mishaps. If a parent has enough self-confidence and personal worth, she or he can stand up to the pressures and frustrations of the child all along the way. The image of a monstrous parent or an indifferent tyrant that arises from a child's imagination has to be recognized and tolerated, with guidance and discipline, as part and parcel of parenthood.

In the atmosphere of hothouse mothering, though, mothers are likely to want only to be admired and/or to succeed according to the image of an idealized mother. The relationship of my client Anne (whom I discussed in earlier chapters) with her daughter suffered from Anne's belief in the "wonders" of motherhood. When Anne's teenage daughter became sternly critical of her mother's preoccupation with an attractive appearance, Anne was unable to hold firm while being honest. Anne wanted "credit" from her daughter for all that she had provided, both as a mother and as a feminist role model. Anne did not want to look straightforwardly at her daughter's envy, competition, criticism, and fear. Anne sugarcoated a lot of what she said to her daughter and used the type of phrasing ("Would you mind if . . ." and "If you don't find it too much trouble . . .") that implied that Anne's requests were too much, that Anne was the hag-bitch.

Her daughter took advantage of Anne's vulnerability and played out the hag-bitch toward Anne, demanding that Anne submit to criticisms, judgments, and pressures. Instead of holding to her own point of view while acknowledging her daughter's hostility, Anne often gave in to her daughter's demands—leaving her daughter feeling much too powerful in her negative emotions.

Anne had to learn how to stand up to her daughter's challenges and to allow her daughter to feel (but not always express) her envy and competition. Anne set limits on what her daughter could say to her but also recognized that her daughter was free to have a range of negative feelings toward her mother. Certainly it was helpful that Anne had a successful career, and a good deal of support for aspects of her identity beyond the role of mother.

Marjorie, by contrast, came to psychotherapy because she had three children under six and was constantly depressed, overwhelmed, and afraid of her aggressive feelings. With a master's in business administration and ten successful years in a lucrative managerial position, she left her career at the age of thirty-three, when she was about to give birth to her first child. Immersed in hothouse mothering, Marjorie had turned all her intelligence to reading about and studying the ideal ways to discipline, toilet train, and raise the perfect child. Now forty, she had lost much of the self-esteem gained by having a world beyond home.

Marjorie's first child, Henry, was a precocious, philosophical little boy who tended to ask penetrating questions about nature, God, and the meaning of life. From her account, Henry was charming and engaging and very popular with his teachers, beginning in nursery school. In many ways Henry was like his articulate father, a charismatic high school principal. Marjorie often felt inferior to six-year-old Henry because she believed that he was much more intelligent and talented than she, and deserved more of her husband's time than she did.

Marjorie nursed Henry until he was fourteen months old and was reluctant to allow him to sleep separately after he was weaned. Naturally, Henry was also reluctant. That was the beginning of a power struggle, which Henry regularly won. Even after Ethan was born, when Henry was almost three years old, Marjorie felt guilty for making Henry sleep in his own bed. By the time Marjorie started psychotherapy, she also had Melaney, who was six months old, but still had not fully demanded that Henry spend the night on his own. Of course there were other power struggles with Henry—over toilet training and discipline and knowledge (he often felt he was more accurate about facts than his mother, and sometimes he was).

Marjorie began therapy after an occasion when she lost control. One day in the family van, with all three children aboard and herself the harried driver, she had hit Henry because he wouldn't let his younger brother take his turn at the favorite window seat. As a result, she feared that she had some fatal flaw in her personality. Moreover, Henry was becoming a tyrant at home, and Marjorie worried that her "aggressive tendencies" were to blame.

Henry was confused and often unhappy. Marjorie's idealization of him had made it impossible for him to behave really badly in public or to express his frustrations openly even at home, so Henry tended to take out his negative feelings on his younger brother. Unbearable things in the psyche are dealt with in a variety of ways, but often they are projected (consciously or unconsciously seen as arising in another) onto someone close at hand. Henry loathed Ethan for his perceived advantages in being younger and for having taken away Mother. Because Henry could not know or say anything directly, he became a tyrant. At home Henry would seem to cut himself off from the rest of the family and make threats and demands, especially regarding Ethan. It was as though Henry felt cut off from his life source in Ethan's presence.

Because Marjorie believed so strongly in Henry's special abilities, she could not imagine how or why he could have become so hostile and aggressive. She tended to deny the seriousness of Henry's recalcitrance *and* to take it on herself, believing that he must have inherited her temper, which she had witnessed in herself only as a developing mother.

Both Marjorie and Henry were absorbed in the archetype of the Divine Child, in which Henry was to behave as an extraordinarily gifted and wise person, and Marjorie was to promote this giftedness by securing him all the best opportunities and possibilities, and by never having to feel really angry with him.

If Henry were to grow up in this atmosphere of hothouse mothering, as an adult he would appear to be absorbed in himself. Others might find him charming or pretentious, but they would resent the attention he always needed. Under the surface, Henry, who might appear quite successful in his work, would be unsure if he was directing his own life.

Growing up as the Divine Child, Henry would feel as though he was always responding to the desires of others instead of his own desire. In place of autonomy, the adult Henry would come to obey an internal source that the psychoanalyst Neville Symington calls the "discordant source": actions and reactions expressing pain and frustration that are not conscious. Sacrificing his autonomy to this discordant source—the pathological residue of a Divine Child complex—Henry would feel that he had no choice in acting out impulses of rage, hostility, and self-destruction (such as addictions or risky behaviors). In place of ordinary modesty and fear, Henry would tend to feel "I can do anything, I am exempt from ordinary constraints. I have the powers of a god."

The Discordant Source

THE SAVAGE NATURE of the discordant source is expressed in a well-known Grimm's fairy tale that describes simply and vividly the consequences of hothouse mothering and projections of the Divine Child. The story of Rumpelstiltskin is retold in my own words here from the tale recorded by the Brothers Grimm around the turn of the nineteenth century. I have transformed the miller of the story into a miller's wife so that she can be the mother of the Divine Child.

RUMPELSTILTSKIN

Once upon a time, a poor miller's wife had a beautiful daughter about whom she boasted a great deal. On one occasion, wanting to make herself seem important, she told the king that her daughter could spin straw into gold. "That is an art that would please me well," replied the king, hoping that he might grow even richer if the miller's wife were telling the truth. "Bring your daughter to my palace tomorrow, and I will put her to the test."

When the girl was brought to him, the king put her into a small room with a spinning wheel, a reel, and many bales of straw. "Set to work now," he commanded. "If you have not spun this straw into gold by tomorrow morning, you must die." With this he locked the room and left the girl alone. She did not know what to do; she had no idea how to spin straw into gold, and she became very afraid and wept.

All at once the door opened and in came a little man who said, "Good evening, mistress. Why are you crying?"

"Because the king has left me here to spin straw into gold and I do not know how to do it."

"What would you give me," said the little man, "if I would do it for you?"

"My necklace," said the girl, handing it over to him.

The little man seated himself at the spinning wheel, and, whirring the wheel, he put in a round of straw and filled a reel up with gold. This went on until daybreak, while the miller's daughter slept. At dawn the little man disappeared at the instant the king appeared at the door. Astonished and delighted at the gold, the king only became greedier.

So he installed the miller's daughter in an even larger room of straw the next night, leaving her alone with the command to spin the straw into gold if she valued her life. Once again the girl wept in fear, and once again the little man appeared. "What will you give me now if I spin this straw into gold?" he asked.

Immediately she answered, "The ring on my finger," and handed it over to him.

The little man took her ring and began to spin, and by morning he had changed all the straw into glittering gold.

The king rejoiced at seeing his riches, but still he was not satisfied. This time he left the girl in an even larger room, but said, "If you succeed in spinning this straw into gold, you shall become my wife." Even though she was only a miller's daughter, he knew he could not find a richer woman in the whole world.

When the girl was alone, the little man came again. "What will you give me now if I spin this straw into gold?"

"I have nothing more to give you," replied the girl with sorrow.

"Then you must promise me that, if you should become queen, you will give me your firstborn child."

Who knows what will happen to me? thought the girl; I doubt that I shall ever be queen. And she agreed to the promise. So, once more, the little man spun the straw into gold.

When the king came the next morning and found what he had wished, he took the miller's daughter in marriage. And so she became the queen.

A year later the queen gave birth to a beautiful child without a thought about her promise to the little man, until suddenly one night he appeared in her room and demanded that she give him what she had promised. Horror-struck, the queen offered the little man all the riches of the kingdom if he would leave her the child.

"Something alive is dearer to me than all the treasures in the world," the little man replied. "But I will give you three days' time; if you can find out my name, then you can keep your child."

The queen thought all day and all night of all the names she knew. She sent a messenger over the country to inquire far and wide for any other names there might be.

When the little man came the next day, the queen began to recite the names she had collected, but to every one the little man replied, "That is not my name." On the second day she made inquiries through the kingdom of the most uncommon and curious names. But when he returned, he always answered, "That is not my name."

On the third day the messenger came back and said, "I have not been able to find a single new name, but I came to the end

of a forest on the high mountain, and there I saw a little house.
Before the house was a fire, around which a ridiculous little
man danced round and round, shouting out, "Today I bake,
tomorrow I brew, the next I'll have the young queen's child.
Ha! glad am I that no one knew that Rumpelstiltskin I am
styled."

The queen was elated. When the little man returned for the
third time, she teased him first with a few names to hear him
say, "No!" Then at last she said, "Perhaps your name is
Rumpelstiltskin."

"The devil has told you that!" cried out the little man. In
his rage, he plunged his right foot so deeply into the earth that
his whole leg went in. And then, in frustration, he pulled at his
left leg so hard with both hands that he tore himself in two.

THIS LITTLE FAIRY TALE portrays the Divine Child complex in two images of the discordant source: the greedy king
and the demanding little man. The miller's wife sacrifices her
only daughter because she wants to seem important to the
king. Who is this king, and how is he connected to Rumpelstiltskin, who does what the king demands of the daughter but
claims for himself everything valuable in her? On the one
hand, the king represents the mother's alliance with patriarchal power—her power complex, her own discordant source.
Rumpelstiltskin, on the other hand, symbolizes the daughter's
Divine Child complex, *her* discordant source. The king and
Rumpelstiltskin are linked together because the daughter
internalizes her mother's needs and develops a "little man
within," who does the king's bidding. This little man replaces
the function of the daughter's autonomy; he produces what the

king desires while the daughter's ego sleeps. Giving over everything of worth to her Divine Child complex is the only way that the daughter can cope with the mother's alliance with patriarchal power.

Naming the Problem

THIS BETRAYAL of the daughter is examined at length in *The Mother-Daughter Revolution: From Betrayal to Power* by Elizabeth Debold, Marie Wilson, and Idelisse Malave. In their own and others' research, they discover that mothers repeatedly transform their daughters' needs for autonomy and power by insisting that daughters conform to the demands of patriarchal institutions. Mothers encourage their daughters to fill the roles of Object of Desire, wife, and mother without helping them to understand the hidden meanings and false powers in these roles.

In the atmosphere of hothouse mothering, daughters as a consequence feel betrayed by their mothers. "Ironically and tragically, mothers are blamed for the very betrayal that they themselves suffered," and the demands they place on their daughters "compromise girls' self-love and integrity. . . . Mothers lose their daughters' trust and, horribly, are rewarded with contempt. These limiting individual strategies perpetuate fear, isolation, and divisiveness." We could say that Rumpelstiltskin is an image of the daughter's genius, of her abilities that she is unable to use for her own development because they are bound to her mother's power needs.

The Divine Child cannot use her normal creative and aggressive impulses to develop her own autonomy. Instead these impulses are channeled into feeding the Divine Child complex, the discordant source. Gradually this complex becomes greedy, hateful, spiteful, and contemptuous because it expresses the internalization of a parent's unconscious strivings for fame, recognition, and power in the world. These negative feelings may manifest themselves only indirectly in the childhood years, as they did in Henry's hostility toward his younger brother. But the grown-up Divine Child expresses his hateful and spiteful feelings in various kinds of hostility and aggression, often directed toward his partners and children but typically disclaimed or denied consciously.

In the story Rumpelstiltskin prophetically says, "Something alive is dearer to me than all the treasures in the world." The developing autonomy of the child is its dearest possession. But the dependent child can easily sacrifice this treasure to the unconscious power needs of those on whom she or he depends. Growing up with a hothouse mother who is self-sacrificing—knowingly or unknowingly wanting to be wanted—can encourage a child to surrender her or his autonomy in exchange for being idealized.

An adult who identified, while growing up, with the Divine Child complex rather than the ego may be unable to see the problems with feeling like the king—superior, special, or unique. Caught up in the complex, the adult believes that she or he is especially *wonderful*, as *wonderful* as an idealized child. Only when the grown-up Divine Child begins to feel the absence of an authentic source, and the presence of a discordant source, will he or she send out a messenger to find the name of the problem.

It is often quite a challenge to get such a person to see what is happening. Even though others, especially family members or close friends, may see and experience the feelings of hostility, greed, superiority, or contempt expressed by the discordant source in the grown-up Divine Child, the individual herself or himself is likely to rationalize or deny them. A telltale sign of this kind of denial is one word, pointed out by the psychoanalyst Symington: the word *just*. The adult Divine Child says, "I was *just* closing the door when you happened to walk into it. I didn't mean to hit you with it." "I was *just* teasing when I said that you shouldn't have that fattening dessert." "I *just* want a little more attention from you." The word *just* is meant to erase the aggressive motive from awareness in both the speaker and the listener.

In the story, the miller's daughter has one true helper: the messenger, who saves her by discovering the name of the discordant source. The messenger symbolizes that aspect of the daughter that wants to discover her authentic truth, the problem that she faces. As the story shows, naming the aggressive motive also means destroying the discordant source and saving one's potential for new development (symbolized as the daughter's baby). The miller's daughter awakens to her genius and begins to make it her own. From then on she will know her desires, her power, and her abilities. In *The Mother-Daughter Revolution* the authors come to the same idea from a different angle: "While the demands on women's lives are intense, the feeling of tiredness that comes from living hard is completely different from the exhaustion of perfection." The miller's daughter found the name of what exhausted her; she will no longer try to live out some alien perfection.

A Mother's Desires

WHEN THE WORSHIPFUL condition of the Divine Child archetype becomes a way of life between mother and child, we have a painful case of the Divine Child complex, which robs both of their authentic development. If this dynamic is allowed to overtake their relationship, especially if the mother is solely responsible for the child, there is a suppression of autonomy and authentic desire in both parties. Sometimes the Divine Child becomes cruelly rejecting of her mother, leaving Mother feeling ashamed and despairing. In such a situation hothouse mothering can become a vicious circle, in which the mother unknowingly tries to meet her self-esteem needs through her child, who is (consciously or unconsciously) intent on attacking the mother's hidden desire for power—the discordant source. This depletes the mother's self-esteem further in a snowballing effect that can bring both parties to a crisis. Mother and child enter into a fierce battle for power, in which the child feels she is fighting for her very life and the mother feels she is fighting for her legitimacy.

Stepping outside the push for hothouse mothering means being able to name the problem and to claim what is "alive" in oneself as "dearer than all the treasures in the world." Claiming the right to sovereignty over your own life, to whatever freedom you can manage in order to pursue a range of responsibilities and tasks as an adult, is the path of healthy mothering. By making good working alliances with mother subs—relatives, neighbors, friends, sitters, partners, and ex-partners—you can share your mothering responsibilities in a way that supports connections between yourself and other adults. Mothering is a demanding, awesome responsibility, and its weight should be carried by many around the child, not by a single individual.

The renewal of hothouse mothering, in the media and among certain experts, is once again increasing the creation of the Divine Child, the inevitable outcome of mothers' isolation in caregiving. Hothouse mothering must be openly opposed if mothers and children are to find the path to authentic sources of autonomy, responsibility, and compassion. Telling the truth about the ambivalence of love and hate in the long dependency of human development is a way of keeping oneself transparent, lively, and honest. Openly resisting and disclaiming the illusion of the perfect mother is a requirement to move ahead in our development as mothers. By acknowledging to others the strains and the strategies of effective mothering, we can form a larger family—beyond the isolation of women and children in the hothouse of the "nuclear" family system.

FIVE

The Material Girl
and the Hungry Ghost

I F A WOMAN CANNOT SUPPORT herself financially, she
does not have the freedom to choose the relationship that
supports her emotionally, for in order to choose the relationship she has to be able to choose to be out of it. Even with
the influence of feminism, many girls and women still believe
that they have more power through appearance, more freedom through seducing power, and greater possibilities through
being desirable than through being responsible for their own
material intentions and welfare. Yet financial dependence in
adulthood is almost always hazardous to psychological health.

Women who come to adulthood as Objects of Desire may
believe that earning a living is a temporary state of affairs until
they can again depend on someone else for all or most of their
material needs. These women yearn for, wish for, and even

expect material security without hard work of their own. Few understand the emotional price they pay in exchange. Because they do not learn the difference between emotional dependence and financial dependence, they cannot be sure if they love their partners or simply need them financially.

Even those of us who earn a living may not understand the symbolism of financial independence because we may feel forced to work for money, believing that some other option (for example, full-time mothering) would lead to greater satisfaction or happiness. We may forget, or never have learned, that paid work does much to keep self-confidence and self-esteem afloat, encouraging us to feel that we are legitimate in a society that regards financial independence as a sign of adulthood. To offer yourself as an equal in a relationship that involves financial support, such as marriage, you need to know that you can support yourself.

As we saw in the last chapter, shared mothering and paid employment benefit the development of both mothers and children. A landmark study by Grace Baruch and Rosalind Barnett elaborated upon these points by showing the importance of paid work for women's development in midlife. These psychologists discovered that the most content and confident midlife women were those who had families *and* paid work. Women who stayed at home, without outside employment, to be full-time mothers often felt pleasure in their relationships but lacked a feeling of competence. Women who worked but did not have intimate or family relationships often felt the opposite—competent but without much pleasure. Women without paid work or children, staying at home as financially dependent housewives, fared the least well in feelings of pleasure and competence. But those women who did *both* mothering and paid work felt both competent and satisfied. Other studies have supported these findings to show that paid work, especially challenging paid work, increases women's satisfaction in life, even when it is combined with the demands of housekeeping and child rearing. In order to feel that satisfaction, though, women have to stop trying to meet ideals of perfection in mothering and housekeeping, and gradually understand how to be Subjects of their own desires.

Taking responsibility for earning income is directly linked to being responsible for and familiar with the world of money. As women develop a better understanding of their financial desires and needs, they learn about limitation and cooperation, about how difficult it is be a "breadwinner" and how much planning goes into even basic financial security.

As the major breadwinner for our family over the last sixteen years, I have enhanced my understanding of this role that is typically filled by men. (In my earlier marriage I was financially dependent; so I know the emotional demands of that condition as well.) I have great empathy for the traditional male position of "provider" because I realize how the experience of earning money for a family's needs is accompanied by a responsibility for others' futures and the fear that should one's health or good fortune fail others would suffer as well. Without the ability to provide financially at least for herself or himself, an adult cannot know the power of financial decision making or benefit from the inventions of necessity that come with earning a livelihood.

Unfortunately many women, younger and older, still believe that appearance and charm, more than achievement and effort, provide financial and emotional security. In striving to be Objects of Desire, they consciously or unconsciously try to seduce power and live out fantasies of dependency through finding a partner who can provide financial security, if not out-right support. Yet many midlife and older women who are financially dependent, and feel hopelessly disconnected from a career or purposeful work identity, are no longer able to imagine themselves as Objects of Desire. Without access to any sources of even imagined power, their unfulfilled longings pursue them through regrets, sadness, and a sense of meaninglessness.

Unequal and Unfree

IN TODAY'S FREE-MARKET economy money equals freedom. This does not mean that earning or inheriting large sums of money is freedom (huge incomes can actually create an encumbrance of greed and attachment to material things) but rather that earning enough money to cover your own life expenses is a symbol of responsible adulthood and an indication that you choose to be where you are because you are free to go. Women still tend to ignore this central message, even though the vast majority of us are employed outside the home.

One reason we may be ignorant of how money is connected to self-determination is that we earn so little of it for the work we do. In the United States we still earn only about seventy-six cents for every dollar men make. Women lack the earning power, status, and decision-making potential that men have in the workplace.

As we have seen throughout earlier chapters, instead of direct compensation and real power, women are promised false power in their roles as desire-awakening maidens, as wives of powerful men, and as mothers. In light of the "power" images that society generates about women's appearance, nurturance, supportiveness, and submission, it's no wonder that women of all ages are confused about the meaning and importance of making their own money.

Women often speak of "working on our relationship" or "doing the work of relating," and they may believe that their emotional skills are worth something on a material level. In our society and many others women are expected to feel and express more emotions than men; they are expected to enhance good feelings and keep intimate ties going. In addition to being encouraged to be Objects of Desire, women are socially reinforced to pursue the power of positive emotions, to keep everyone happy. Trading on good feelings and making assertions of "relational superiority," some women make claims for equal worth in marriages where they earn much less income than their husbands, or no income at all.

Ironically, this work of love is financially rewarded only in divorce. Sociologist Marcia Millman has described two such cases in her analysis of the role of money in the family.

> One woman, divorcing a clinically depressed husband, claims she earned a share of his inheritance because she kept him sane and functioning over many years. Another woman, dumped by her husband, argues in court that she deserves half of the marital property, though she didn't work for wages, because her husband was a "full-time job."

What might have been perceived as love going into the marriage is translated by the woman as money coming out.

As problematic as it may seem, making money means power and freedom of self-determination throughout long stretches of adult life. When love and trust are no longer the heart of an intimate relationship, people turn to the signs of power to evaluate and protect their personal worth.

Female Desire in the Workplace

WHAT THEN HAPPENS to the majority of us who earn money and work full-time? Do we automatically have greater access to positive evaluations of ourselves? Obviously not, because the workplace is yet another setting in which male rules dictate most of our conduct and the means for our moving up in the power hierarchy. If you work in an organization or institution, it's more likely than not that men are in charge at the highest levels and have been there from the outset. If you work for a woman-owned-and-operated business, or for yourself, you may have different circumstances, but you still have to conform to certain rules of conduct that permeate our society. Even working for yourself means interacting with other organizations and social systems that operate according to the old rules of patriarchy. As we have seen, women are openly invited to want to be wanted—to be desirable, nice, inspiring—and are threatened with being known as hag-bitches if they directly claim power and authority. In the workplace this situation makes for an impossible balancing act.

A number of years ago I presented a lecture on gender differences to an audience of high-powered international executives. Most of the women in the audience were wives of the executives, but there was a handful of women executives present. After my presentation I was harassed by male respondents who criticized me, without referring to anything I presented, for what they interpreted as my desire to eliminate sex differences and "make women into men." No matter how I answered, the men in this group would not allow themselves to understand what I was saying about the importance of female-male partnership and equality for work and family in our future. They wanted to label me the hag-bitch and avoid or trivialize the research and ideas I had presented.

After about an hour, an articulate and obviously passionate woman from India stood up and spoke about how cruel and troubling her life as a corporate leader and a woman of color had been over the past twenty years. As an international leader she was frequently exposed to the double bind of female authority: you're damned if you take direct authority, and you're damned if you don't. Because she found that she could not be an Object of Desire *and* a competent leader, she had decided early on to be strong, direct, and tough in her influential position. So she was frequently called a bitch and blamed for being rigid and demanding. She spoke of her commitment to her own goals over the years, and of her widespread achievements. Yet she wondered if she could continue in her position because she felt emotionally depleted from the constant blame and criticism. She feared that she might soon surrender her leadership position in order to achieve greater peace of mind. I thanked her with a deep sense of appreciation for her frankness and support. The men acted as though they had heard nothing.

We expect females at work and in public domains to be self-deprecating, to want to avoid conflicts, and to want to be liked—even when these attitudes mean being less effective. When women do not behave as expected, they are frequently attacked. Linguist Deborah Tannen describes the dilemma of a woman at work, whether the work is challenging and well-paid or menial and underpaid: "Everything she does to enhance her assertiveness risks undercutting her femininity, in the eyes of others. And everything she does to fit expectations of how a woman should talk risks undercutting the impression of competence she makes."

The socialization and habits connected with being the Object of Desire translate into certain styles and tendencies of female communication that are in sharp contrast with male styles, especially in the workplace. Many years ago I saw in psychotherapy a successful female lawyer who labeled the male way of handling power at work as Boasting, Roasting, and Toasting. Men boast about their accomplishments, tease and razz each other in playful and jockeying ways, and praise and credit other men for competence and ideas—often remaining silent about or ignoring the same things in women.

In working with this client, I eventually labeled women's comparable styles and tendencies as Caring, Sharing, and Baring (our souls). My client was tired of both styles. She resented male power posturing, but she also disliked what she saw as the overly personal, indirect approach of female power. We expect women to avoid boasting, and by and large they do so, playing down their talents and abilities and appearing from their speech to be less confident than men. Women tend to use the conversational rituals of "I'm sorry" and "thanks" when these statements are not literally meaningful but induce a feeling of closeness between speakers. This kind of conversational ritual makes sense only when the speakers share the belief that it is a ritual about closeness, not about having less power. The combination of a self-deprecating manner, a desire to talk about personal issues at work, and a need to share feelings may enhance relationships among women, but it does not carry over as effective communication with men—especially if a woman's competence and authority are meant to be part of the message.

Most studies of women's conversational styles show women

to be more indirect in asking people to do things, just as I described in Anne's tendency to say "Would you mind if" or "Would you like to." In American society this manner is often labeled manipulative or deceptive, but in other societies— such as the Japanese—this style is thought to be more mature than a direct, abrupt request. Such indirect statements do not, then, necessarily mean a lack of conviction or authority, but they are read this way in American work settings.

In America women do better to speak directly and make claims for what they know—calmly, without blaming others— than to attempt to be liked by exemplifying feminine manners and then be overlooked for raises and rewards. Although they may be labeled hag-bitches at first, they will generally become better known for the work they do than for the way they look, what they wear, or how nice they are.

The Problem with Competence

WOMEN FREQUENTLY BELIEVE that competence leads directly to power, authority, and material rewards in the work setting. It does not. What leads to power is self-promotion, making the right connections, and being self-confident— based on actual skills and knowledge, not posturing. Although we may fear that self-promoting will provoke resentment from peers, sound boastful, or demean others' contributions, we must step outside the double bind of female authority because it will undermine all of our efforts to be effective. As Tannen describes it, when a woman is in a position of influence and leadership, "there is an expectation that she will be unfeminine, negative, or worse. . . . And these prevalent images ambush professional women as they seek to maintain their

careers as well as their personal lives." It is difficult but important to claim repeatedly what we know and how effective we
are, without blaming others for not seeing these qualities automatically. If you surrender to demands to be feminine and lik-
able, you will undermine your authority and power at work and
ultimately lose the possibility of moving ahead. Yet, like the
woman executive I described earlier, we are inevitably at risk
for being labeled bitches if we stand on our own authority. For
this reason it is essential to find ongoing supports and encour-
agement from friends (at work, if possible) who can see the
reality of the double bind, confirm your effectiveness, and recognize your right to be known for your performance rather
than your appearance.

When women do not fit stereotypical images of self-
deprecating femininity, they are more likely to become self-
determining and responsible for their own development. I am
not suggesting that women become bullies or take on the
Boasting, Roasting, and Toasting that men in power embrace.
Rather I am saying that women need to be aware that they
work in a patriarchal society, in which power does not come
directly from being competent and in which conversational
styles signal gender stereotypes. Speaking as the confident
Lady Ragnell, who says, "I have the answer," is not identical
with boasting about yourself. It is an authentic and truthful
way of representing your knowledge and skill. To be the Subjects of our desires in the workplace, we have to develop a settled,
centered, and honest style of communication about strengths
and weaknesses, as well as a strategic understanding of the
workings and styles of male power.

Standing up, making ourselves known, and being truly confident are ways of transforming female desire from wanting to

be wanted into wanting to be seen and heard as sources of innovation, successful ideas, and hard work. Knowing that we can depend on ourselves in the workplace and develop gradually to meet reasonable goals for ourselves does not mean that we increase our independence from others or need others less. It simply means that we can depend on others in a mature way and that we can make choices for ourselves rather than feel resentful and overwhelmed by others' needs.

Equality in Trust

MATURE DEPENDENCE, a term I borrow from the psychoanalyst Ronald Fairbairn, means a style of dependence in adult life in which you are grateful, appreciative, and free to depend openly because you know the importance of give-and-take and are dependable as well as dependent. This style of dependence should be a goal in all aspects of adult life, both in the workplace and at home.

Mature dependence is in stark contrast to both the immature, clinging dependence that is exemplified by an infant or young child and the anxious, defensive independence that is exemplified by the adolescent struggling for emancipation. A financially dependent adult—female or male—often feels immaturely dependent or defensively independent (staking out unnecessary claims of doing it "my way") rather than maturely dependent.

Instead of believing that we develop from being dependent to being independent human beings, I believe that we develop our ability to be dependent—from early infant dependence through the dependence of childhood and the defensive pseudoindependence of adolescence to the final mature dependence of adulthood. Everyone has the potential to develop through dependence, but only those who can work through earlier stages of dependence to later ones will actually succeed. There is no real independence for humans, because we always need and depend on others; independence is an illusion.

Mature dependence is a developmental achievement then, available only to those who can establish a mutual rhythm of give-and-take with a partner or friend. One has to be an equal in order to respect that other as much as the self (not more, not less). A key part of mature dependence is trust.

Pooling our resources in a relationship signals the willingness to trust and usually communicates the desire to function as equals, even when one partner earns a lot more money than the other. Couples who pool their financial resources are more likely to stay together than those who do not. Only in couples where women make twice or three times their male partners' income have I heard confusion and hiding about who makes what in the common pool of finances. Obviously, honesty and knowledge are necessary ingredients in pooling resources, so that both partners know what each contributes and can fully appreciate each other's efforts and situations.

Lesbian couples can teach us about trust and equality in money. In a study by the sociologists Philip Blumstein and Pepper Schwartz, lesbians were sensitive and honest about the inferior financial status of women in the workplace and accepted the limitations of each other's earning capacities. If one partner was better educated or of a higher social class, or simply luckier in finding well-paid employment, she supported the other partner rather than criticizing her for making less money. Lesbians appeared to appreciate and even cherish what each partner brought to the sharing of finances—both partners earning whatever income they could, typically each enough to be self-supporting.

Women in heterosexual relationships, especially in marriages, can feel confused and frustrated about how to express financial equality and mature dependence. When Cheryl, from Chapter One, came to psychotherapy she was in a relationship with Brad, a younger man who was still a college student. I talked about how he took advantage of her greater income although he refused to commit to her emotionally. Many women have told me that they prefer to keep individual checking and savings accounts and to have what is clearly their "own" money so that they don't have to answer to anyone about earning or spending.

Such financial separation means that chit lists and power struggles about who owes whom what can interfere with intimate relating. Women are generally not as comfortable dealing with money as men, because we have not been socialized to see doing so as part of our adult responsibilities. I believe that some of our desire to protect individual earnings, and to keep accounts separate, is related to the prevalence of shame in female development.

Shame is a self-conscious emotion (like pride, envy, embarrassment, guilt, and self-pity) that arises in the second year of life, after the infant is able to distinguish its own body-self reliably from other things. The difference between "in here" and "out there," between "mine" and "yours," has to be well-organized before we can feel conscious of "me and mine" versus "you and yours."

When it comes to succeeding at having and managing one's own money, I believe that many women want the freedom from having to be on view in their earning and spending habits. Like Ragnell hiding in the woods, they may still be trapped in shame. They may also, however, have a legitimate problem with trusting a partner who is not responsive and responsible. Women like Cheryl, who have been reticent to pool their income with partners like Brad, may be expressing their unwillingness to trust through the unwillingness to pool finances. If you are unwilling to share openly and honestly on a financial level, perhaps you need to examine whether you trust your partner on emotional and sexual levels. Financial trust should come naturally on the heels of emotional and sexual trust, as long as we are not dominated by shame.

The Subject (or Object?) of Shopping

THE INTERTWINING OF emotional and financial trust is perhaps nowhere more difficult for heterosexual couples than in the area of shopping and consumerism. I have come across all kinds of crude explanations for what is often regarded as an almost exclusively female "drive" to shop—as though it were biologically ordained from women's supposed adaptation as hunter-gatherers. There is no doubt that shopping is a major material domain that haunts women's relationship to money, but I have discovered that women historically are linked to shopping, as men are linked to sports, as a means to develop the feeling of being in charge of one's own being, knowing how and when to make decisions.

Beginning in the late Victorian era and continuing through the explosion into full-blown consumerism by the 1920s, women were invited to feel a kind of liberation in shopping for personal items, as I showed in Chapter Two. With the onset of an American middle class in the latter part of the nineteenth century, shopping and consumer spending emerged as an important part of female life. Women, who had been excluded from any significant economic activity, suddenly became central to practices and theories of modern consumerism: how to seduce shoppers to buy more than they needed.

Earlier dark and unattractive dry goods stores were gradually transformed into glamorous, well-lit, exciting department stores. By the beginning of the twentieth century these department stores, especially in New York, were considered almost a cultural achievement. Macy's, Wanamaker's, and Altman's were among the first to draw customers by creating beautiful environments. Women came to these stores for pleasure, conversation, and to avail themselves of a range of commodities—particularly to substitute much-touted ready-made garments for handmade goods.

Once ready-to-wear became widely available, the department stores began to foster an extravagant demand for new clothes and eventually other personal products, such as cosmetics, attempting to keep their sales volume greater than overhead costs. Before department stores there had been little fashion for women who were not among the most privileged classes. Now keeping up with fashion would make all the difference to an ordinary middle-class woman, who could never, of course, keep up with an image that was constantly being manipulated and changed by designers and retailers in order to create consumption.

To participate in this new and stimulating form of consumption, and simply to enjoy themselves, middle-class women increased their number of shopping days to the extent that they were shopping every third or fourth day. So women and department stores became partners in a new social development, a profound cultural transformation in which both women and stores were caught up in the murky business of creating desires and longings that can never be satisfied.

The woman shopper was being seduced into an atmosphere that promised her the power of choice: to be the Subject of her own desires. Created by male retailers specifically for women's needs and desires—and widely criticized by husbands, preachers, and doctors—these new shopping environments became the first material world to promise women some form of individual freedom.

Shopping was designed for women as an intoxicating mix of promises to be both the Object *and* the Subject of Desire. Choosing material things, especially clothes, women could follow their own desires, at the same time keeping up with the cultural image of the desire-awakening maiden, the seductive youthful female. No wonder even feminist women like myself can still be attracted by the smells and sights of a department store! Here was perhaps the first widespread cultural development that was designed especially with the female as Subject in mind, and meant also to address all the stereotypes of cultural femininity and women's wanting to be wanted.

Our contemporary shopping malls and megadiscount stores are only the extensions and continuations of the life of the department store, and they now appeal to women at all income levels. By producing products that need to be replaced quickly, and by creating need that does not arise from necessity, modern consumerism appeals especially to women because it appears to offer choices. When we make choices we feel we have a measure of control. Shopping offers an escape from our resentment at having given in to others' wishes and desires, *and* it promises that we can mold our images to fit the current cultural muse, the perfect mother, or the competent boss.

But because women are *not* in control of either the fashion industry or other large retail enterprises, they have once again been tricked into believing they have power as Objects of Desire. Retailers seduce us to buy freedom when no freedom is available. Instead of freedom, modern consumerism creates more desire, even compulsion.

Unless we are conscious of the endless cycle of desire—need arising from the memory of pleasure—we can become driven by desires that overtake all other activity. Shopping was designed to create and multiply desires for things and images. Most shoppers are unconscious or somewhat unconscious that shopping environments, especially beautiful and sensually pleasing ones, create need and breed desire.

If you are bound to shopping or fashion, or simply want a lot of consumer goods, you will find that new purchases don't satisfy desire, except for a brief moment. The effect of the purchase inevitably fades, and desire emerges for the next thing. Women who suffer from feelings of shame or envy, who feel they are empty of resources to make life meaningful, are especially likely to turn to consumerism and its false promise to fill the black hole inside.

Hungry Ghosts

IN BUDDHISM, as I mentioned in my introduction, there is an account of different forms of existence that are symbolized as unique realms on the Wheel of Life. These realms can be understood as actual places, states of mind, or both. The realm of the Hungry Ghosts is where beings are driven by unfulfilled desires. It is a hell realm, although not the worst hell. Often the Hungry Ghosts are described as trying to satisfy unfulfilled desires connected to lifetimes that have already passed and cannot be relived.

Hungry Ghosts are depicted as humanlike creatures with long throats that are so narrow and raw that swallowing produces unbearable pain. Their huge, distended bellies are unable to digest any nourishment, and attempts to gratify themselves only yield more intense hunger. Hungry Ghosts cannot take joy in the experiences of everyday life but are obsessed with achieving complete release from the pains of their past, unaware that their desires are unattainable. The empty, insatiable nature of Hungry Ghosts is painfully expressed by women who are caught in the material world of shopping.

Cassandra, a wealthy woman of sixty-five, was living alone with four cats and a lot of depression when she first came to see me in psychotherapy. In her youth she had been a great beauty, and she had been married (and divorced) three times, always to successful businessmen who had problems with alcohol or drug dependency. She had five children—now grown—whom she had raised without emotional support from their fathers.

While her children were young, Cassandra had worked as a weaver and quilter and had a business of her own, selling her craft. She did not make much money at it, not enough to support herself, but she enjoyed the work, and her husbands always supplied enough child support and alimony to provide a very comfortable life for her and her children. Cassandra thought it was her part of the script to provide a nurturing home environment, to be a good cook, to grow lovely gardens, and to look beautiful. She never imagined anything like a career for herself, nor did she think she had missed out on anything by not having one.

Cassandra came to me because she was very distressed by her propensity to shoplift. Mostly she stole expensive items of clothing and extravagant jewelry—pieces she could not afford. She stole only from large department stores that she felt could easily absorb the loss, and she made sure to spend money in those same stores, places in which she was well-known and liked by salesclerks. Several times she had been caught, although usually she was treated gently by the police. She was deeply ashamed of her behavior but also confessed to me that it was extremely exciting: "It's almost sexual. I get weak in the knees and sweat all over, and then I am so overjoyed when I get out of the store. Free! I feel that I have gotten back at a few of those people who have cheated me out of a good life—like my husbands. I know the owners of the stores are men like my husbands; some I have even known personally. I feel excited that I have taken something from them."

But Cassandra would become very ashamed of her behavior within hours after her triumphs. Many times she would give away what she had stolen, either to her children or to the poor. Telling me about her excitement in stealing was difficult for Cassandra, who saw herself as deeply honest with a lot of integrity.

Like her namesake, Cassandra was often the person in her family who could intuit the truth of a situation but could not convince others of what she saw. In her adult years, especially in her marriages, Cassandra often spoke the truth, but she did it with so much blame and resentment that her husbands, even her children, failed to believe her. Known for her beautiful appearance, Cassandra was also known as a "hysterical woman" who was frequently on edge in some social situations—"just trying to get across my point," she would say while holding forth in monologues in which she brought too much evidence and argument to bear.

Over the years Cassandra had come to see that shoplifting meant something more than a mere addiction to her. She could see that it expressed something she wanted in her life.

But instead of investigating what that might be, she had hung on to her resentment over losing her relationships and her beauty and continued to shoplift.

Cassandra was living in the realm of Hungry Ghosts. With unmet needs to be validated, and a painful longing to be taken seriously, she tried to retaliate against the "powerful" parents/husbands of her psychological complexes by stealing resources from them. She was constantly empty and lonely, and often felt like retaliating against others' successes and freedoms, even those of her children.

Between episodes of shoplifting, Cassandra could find no meaning in her life. She had few social activities and often found herself alone in front of the television with a pint of ice cream for company. Recently she had inherited almost a million dollars through her father's estate, which terrified her. She did not want the responsibility for the money, nor did she have any idea about what she could do with it. She felt ashamed and undeserving, not only because she had openly despised her father but also because Cassandra felt she was fundamentally a loser, a criminal. She deeply disliked herself, calling herself "a fat, old thief" and claiming that she had been ruined by her husbands' demands and addictions.

Pathologies of Female Material Desire

THREE PATHOLOGIES OF FEMALE material desire are bound together in their meanings, and sometimes in their occurrences: compulsive shopping and overspending; shoplifting; and binge eating. All three of these problems involve Hungry Ghost fantasies—obsessions with desires of attaining complete release from the pain of the past, unaware that these obsessions can never be satisfied through material means.

Shoplifting costs American retailers roughly $10 billion per year, and it is spreading in almost epidemic proportions all over the country, from urban centers to small towns. The overwhelming number of shoplifters in urban department stores and malls are female, mostly middle-class and upper-middle-class, who steal things for excitement, not because they need them or because the things are especially useful. For some Hungry Ghosts the high of shoplifting is almost unrivaled among addictions.

In a recent magazine article a young woman was quoted as saying that shoplifting is a tougher habit to break than heroin. She steals not only clothes and smaller items but also household appliances, like her TV and freezer. "I can go two to three weeks without drugs, but not a day goes by that I don't shoplift. I saw a shrink. He put me on Paxil; he thought it would help me. But I'm not depressed. I just like to steal a lot." This woman's desires to steal are conscious and have probably substituted for doing other exciting or meaningful things with her life. She has chosen the quick fix and tries to quell her pain and frustration through acquiring something new.

Cassandra used stealing to respond to resentment and loss, to frustration and fears about her future. Many women shoplifters are acting out a loss, according to clinical psychologist Will Cupchik, whose book *Why Honest People Shoplift* has become the focus of support groups and web sites to address the Hungry Ghost longings of episodic shoplifters. He believes that women are stealing because they have unconscious desires they have not recognized: losses they have not satisfactorily addressed, hurt and anger from relationships that have been abusive or unsatisfying. They feel victimized by a variety of people whom they want to get back at through stealing. As the psychiatrist Mark Epstein says of Hungry Ghosts, they "have uncovered a terrible emptiness within themselves" and "cannot see the impossibility of correcting something that has already happened."

Those of us who don't identify with Cassandra might find ourselves all too familiar with the second pathology of female material desire: compulsive shopping. Compulsive shopping has been around for a long time, at least since department stores. In 1860, when Abraham Lincoln was elected President of the United States, it became clear that his wife, Mary Todd, had a bad habit of overspending. During her tenure in the White House she made over eleven major forays into New York to enlarge her wardrobe and redecorate the White House, vastly overspending her budget, which was a great distress to her husband. Another more recent First Lady, Jacqueline Kennedy Onassis, dismayed both of her husbands, President John Kennedy and Aristotle Onassis, with her lavish expenditures on clothes and furnishings. Charlotte Curtis of *The New York Times* is quoted as saying, "Jackie's expenditure of $50,000 for clothes in 16 months after Jack Kennedy's election was about two-thirds of his income from the trust fund his father had set up for him and his other children." Princess Diana, another icon Object of Desire of our century, was a well-known clotheshorse and jet-setter who eventually auctioned off much of her extravagant wardrobe and apparently pledged herself to a simpler lifestyle, although the nature of that future life was not clear by the time she died in Paris—after shopping there all day.

But it is not only the rich and famous who overspend and feel driven to shop for expensive or unnecessary items. There are estimates that up to 8.1 percent of the American population falls into the category of compulsive buying. Of this group, 80 to 92 percent are female, ranging in age from eighteen to thirty-nine years.

Compulsive buying is distinguished from ordinary shopping and overspending by the following criteria: frequent preoccupations with buying or impulses to buy that are experienced as irresistible and senseless; frequent buying of more than can be afforded, and of items that are not needed; and shopping for longer periods than intended. These impulses interfere significantly with work and family life, and often can result in severe financial problems, such as bankruptcy.

Compulsive shoppers turn to stores when they feel sad, lonely, angry, frustrated, hurt, or irritable. The vast majority report feeling happy or powerful when they are shopping, although this feeling is followed by depression when they realize how much money they have spent. They prefer to shop alone and have more credit cards, rely on them more, and have more credit-card debt than others do. One study showed that normal buyers pay about 22 percent of their income to debts, while the average figure for compulsive buyers is 46 percent.

Like our shopping foremothers, compulsive buyers describe their pleasure in shopping as enhanced by the colors, sounds, lighting, displays, and smells of stores, as well as the textures of clothing. Some compulsive shoppers describe their experiences as sexually exciting, although they may feel terrible remorse when they get their packages home.

But one does not have to be compulsive to fall into the shopping trap. Researchers surveying a group of both male and female "impulse buyers" who did not all fully meet the criteria of compulsive buyers were especially interested to discover whether there was some kind of personality trait associated with impulsive buying, something more enduring than a transitory mood. They discovered that women were more likely to be impulse shoppers than men. The female impulse buyer had either high materialistic desires and/or high discrepancy between her ideal self-image and her perceived self-image—something the researchers called self-discrepancy. They concluded,

> It is well established that there are more female than male compulsive buyers, and this pattern appears to be reflected in our more normal sample in impulse buying. One possibility is that shopping is a self-completion strategy that is easily available to women (either through socialization or opportunity) while other self-completion strategies may be more available to men (e.g., alcoholism or participation in sports).

I have talked about Anne many times, and she is a good example of an impulse buyer who is not pathological in her need to shop but who uses shopping to shore up low self-esteem. When Anne has finished a long day at work, or sometimes when she has a longer lunch hour than usual, she finds herself wandering through her favorite clothes and lingerie shops without a clear intention. When she and I talked about these occasions in greater detail, we discovered that they almost always came on the heels of a disappointment at work, at home, or with a friend in which Anne felt she gave up her own needs in favor of someone else's. Rather than address these events through understanding her problems with self-determination, with wanting to be wanted, Anne unintentionally sought shopping as a self-soothing activity. Sometimes she *was* soothed by a couple of hours in the stores, but more often she was frustrated when she got home and found she had spent more time and money than she could afford.

Like Anne, many of us use shopping to soothe our feelings when we feel out of control in other areas of our lives. And we also feel disappointed and frustrated when we find we have purchased too much, spent too much time, or simply wasted our energies. Like Hungry Ghosts who are obsessed with stopping the pain inside and unaware of what is happening in the present moment, we wander about in the shopping realm, an environment that was designed precisely to increase our belief that we can satisfy desires that can never be fulfilled. That hunger inside, often described by women clients as a black hole that consumes everything into its despair, can also lead to overeating, the third pathology of female material desire.

Binge eating, something I discussed briefly in relation to Princess Diana in Chapter One, may occur in women's lives as an occasional problem or as a severe addiction. Chronic binge eaters consume large quantities of food, enough to make themselves sick. Some vomit, others don't. Like the Hungry Ghost who is known to suffer terrible indigestion, Cassandra would eat large quantities of pretzels and ice cream, then go to bed with a terrible stomachache and cry herself to sleep. Food, like shopping, creates a physical sensation that seems to fill up the emptiness inside. In this way we can consider binge eating a material desire; food is an aspect of the material world.

The three pathologies of female desire are often found in tandem or in unison. That is, shoplifting, compulsive shopping, and binge eating often affect the same woman, either over time or simultaneously. The rest of us, who are not pathologically addicted to these activities, may find that we crave either things or food in the face of painful, unfulfilled desires.

Longing for Abundance

SOME WOMEN TURN to material goods for comfort or revenge for lost loves or other losses. Other women are desperate to have the newest fashion or thing of beauty that is meant to increase their attractiveness or compensate for what has gone wrong. Persuaded by patriarchal culture to seek power in the feminine roles of muse, mother, and wife, they discover no real choice or power there, and they turn the blame and resentment on themselves. Instead of recognizing the problem with making an image rather than a self, instead of learning to know their desires and develop self-knowledge, women continue to turn to old habits that momentarily relieve the pain.

All three pathologies of female material desire have in common the experience of unfulfilled cravings and painful emptiness. Mark Epstein says that "longing for inexhaustible abundance is very common in the Western psyche, where it masquerades under the heading of 'low self-esteem.'" If by midlife a woman does not have a clear sense of her worth and her own desires, then she will have developed a black hole in place of an authentic self. The hole is the Hungry Ghost, always craving to fulfill impossible desires and unable to be content in the moment.

As we've learned, female power is not appearance, nor is the seduction of power any guarantee of material security. Nor can material success bring us inner security, contentment, and peace. Cassandra had to learn all three of these things successively in her psychotherapy. First, she had to look back at her own wishes for power and control that were projected onto others. She had to acknowledge how important her appearance had been to her and how much she had counted on it to bring her what she wanted in life. She also had to recognize that her children could never give her a life of purpose and meaning; they were passing through her life in search of lives of their own. Letting go of her attempts to control two of her grown daughters was significant progress in Cassandra's rather quick improvement in therapy.

Then she and I looked squarely at the meaning of her inheritance. She had been born her father's daughter, and she had received this money through that birth, not through any particular work of her own. Yet it was a part of her individual karma, a circumstance of her birth that only she could develop and mold. In our work together, deeply examining what Cassandra's authentic needs and desires were, she decided to buy some rural property and open an animal sanctuary for both wild and domestic animals. Cassandra's cats had been a great comfort to her over the years, and she felt deeply for animals who were abandoned or abused. In many ways Cassandra identified with wounded animals because she felt that they, like herself, often trusted too much or in the wrong places.

Organizing the plans for her sanctuary became Cassandra's major project. No longer did she feel empty, and no longer was she drawn to shoplifting or binge eating. In fact, Cassandra began to describe her inheritance as a spiritual offering from her father, something that she could use to transform her life into an existence of deeper connections and greater joy. When we talked about the possibility of Cassandra shoplifting at some future time when something would go awry, she gave her solemn word that she would not. She said she understood that the shoplifting was an impossible career: it never led to real joy, and it always put her at risk for shame.

As Cassandra came closer to making her project a reality

and felt wholly engaged by getting to know both the physical surroundings of her sanctuary and the animals that would be sheltered there, a wonderful transformation took place. She experienced herself as a worthwhile human being who was living in the way she felt she was meant to. We called this feeling of groundedness "spiritual nourishment," and I thought of the Bodhisattva of Compassion, who offers the Hungry Ghosts spiritual refreshment.

In each of the realms of the Wheel of Life there is a helpful figure (a *bodhisattva*, or saintly helper) who challenges the beings there to wake up and liberate themselves to greater freedom, eventually to full enlightenment—a state of alert wakefulness, living in the moment. In the human realm this helpful figure is Buddha Shakyamuni, a human being who founded the religion of Buddhism and taught its practices and theories for forty-nine years after his Supreme Enlightenment, more than twenty-five hundred years ago. According to Buddhism, a Buddha (a perfectly enlightened being) appeared in the human realm specifically to show humans how to liberate themselves from suffering. Only we can awaken ourselves to how we create distressing and painful situations through our desires and hidden intentions. Only we can change. The Buddha is a spiritual psychotherapist who invites us to learn how to free ourselves from greed, hatred, and ignorance.

What is the helpful figure in the realm of Hungry Ghosts? It's the Bodhisattva of Compassion, holding out a bowl filled with objects that are symbolic of spiritual nourishment. The Ghosts must recognize that their cravings and fantasies will never be fulfilled by material things but only by pursuing a spiritual path. In simply showing the Ghosts spiritual nourishment, the bodhisattva reminds them of the inherent need to lead a meaningful life on a deeper level, to feel connected to others, and to develop compassion for oneself and others. In Zen Buddhism this is called "rousing the thought of Enlightenment." The aching longings of Hungry Ghosts express a need for spiritual nourishment, the only kind of nourishment that can really satisfy their emptiness.

Spiritual Nourishment

SO WHAT IS THIS spiritual nourishment, and how does it affect our material desires? If you are a Material Girl, does that mean you are destined to live as a Hungry Ghost? I have come to believe that the questions surrounding how we earn and use money are especially useful for girls and women. They are often the bridge to understanding that a sense of inner emptiness and lack of worth may be the door to a spiritual path, may raise the question of what it means to be human, to be responsible for your intentions in creating a life.

Our Western material longings for inexhaustible abundance too often substitute for the experience of a core self connected to others and sustained by our own intentions. On the one hand, it is useful to be financially responsible, so that you can be free to discriminate emotional dependence (and develop mature dependence) from financial dependence. On the other hand, our material longings, especially if they are confused with a sense of self or worth, can tie us into the murky business of creating desires and longings that cannot be satisfied.

Girls and women in our society are faced with the complicated and confusing task of knowing the difference between making a living and being a Material Girl. The former leads to development through necessity, but the latter is a joke played on us by the shopping business. There is nothing wrong with shopping and spending in themselves; they can be great delights, if they are recognized as momentary pleasures. When shopping is kept human-size, it is a matter of choice, not compulsion.

Earning your own living, cooperating as a financial partner in a relationship, and solving money problems will free you to be a self-determining adult in the material world, but excessive spending and attachment to material things will bind you to a realm of impossible wishes based on emptiness. Even if you are caught in the realm of Hungry Ghosts, however, you can awaken to the reality of your unfulfilled desires, recognize your ghostliness, and follow your true spiritual yearnings.

Spiritual yearnings may take the form of wanting more insight into the ways you create conflict and suffering in your life, so that you can live in greater harmony with yourself and others. They may take the form of desires for some enduring purpose or meaning, beyond earning a living and raising a family. They may take the form of wanting to help others change the conditions of materialism, greed, and power mongering that bring so much pain to the human and natural worlds of our planet. Whatever the forms, the yearnings of Hungry Ghosts are hidden desires for fulfillment beyond the material world.

Becoming aware of your psychological complexes, especially those that interfere with self-determination in your material life, is often a first step toward becoming a Subject of your own spiritual desires. We humans can know our own intentions and direct our lives responsibly and compassionately. This is a great privilege, but many of us remain trapped in the realm of Hungry Ghosts, forsaking life as intentional human beings.

To live as intentional human beings, discovering and following our spiritual longings, is a specific challenge for women in patriarchal society. All the great religions of the world have created symbols, rituals, and meanings that have been used to oppress women and to turn us away from understanding our own experiences. Still, this is a period in which women are encountering these traditional religions in a distinctly feminist way and are shaping new traditions as well. In the next chapter I will address the challenge of self-determination for women following a spiritual path or a religion, aroused from the vague yearnings of a Hungry Ghost.

SIX

The Spiritual Problem of Giving Your Self Away

WE ALL LONG FOR SOMETHING to take us outside ourselves, beyond our discontent. As we saw in the last chapter, we can be duped into believing that material things will fill the black hole of inner emptiness. Women, especially, can get lost in the realm of Hungry Ghosts, wanting and acquiring more and more material things in an attempt to shore up appearance and security in the process of aging.

The great religions teach us that only spiritual nourishment can truly satisfy our longing for security and inner peace. Yet for centuries this spiritual nourishment—particularly in the form of meaning, purpose, and connection—has been available only in the packaging of religious language and images in which women were almost never self-determining Subjects.

Only recently women have begun to influence our religious traditions and practices in the roles of leaders, teachers, and thinkers.

As a Jungian psychoanalyst, I regard spiritual development as a necessary component of a healthy, effective life as a human being. By spiritual development I mean a lifetime engagement with a transcendent source that is intimate and Other. This development begins in childhood, out of our dependence on others. In our early years we are awed by our parents and elders, whose power seems supreme: Who are They? They are our earliest encounter with an Otherness that sustains and protects us. The images and meanings that we accrue in those early contacts with Otherness introduce us to, or block us from, a later respect for and interest in the transcendent.

If we mature emotionally as we grow older, we come to see that we are responsible for sustaining and protecting ourselves. This is a fearful prospect. Some adults never wholly assume this responsibility but continue to hope for protection and favors from a powerful Otherness (God, Goddess, divinities). Their spiritual development remains in a childish form.

Assuming responsibility for our own (and eventually others') lives is a transformative event that should lead to the next phase of spiritual development: What is my purpose here? How do I fit into the intimate Otherness of family, society, the world? If we discover a satisfactory answer to this question—and some may not, the search may be lifelong—then we naturally turn our attention to the last, great spiritual mystery: Who are we? Why are we here? Mature spirituality is the honing of integrity, wisdom, and transcendence in regard to the question of what it means to be human within the Otherness of our universe.

Traditionally, religions guided spiritual development; symbolic connections were regulated by images and processes that were automatically made available to the developing child as well as the mature adult. But in our era development is more individual, random, and easily derailed. Mystery and awe are now thought to arise more from a stroll under the night sky or a climb to a panoramic mountain view than from religions and responsibility. Our only widespread symbolic connections come from TV and movies.

Many of us question whether we need religion in today's world. Some feminists have doubted its usefulness for women because the world's religions are sexist in many of their basic practices. Over the centuries religions have cast women as selfless mothers and protectors of virtue in the family, as childish beings who need protection and guidance themselves, or as sexual and sensual temptresses and deceivers of men. As we've seen, such roles emerged from patriarchy and can be found in all aspects of life, but they have been rationalized and defended by theology and religion. So if religions have been so harmful to women, why is spirituality important to female self-determination? And further, how can women have access to spiritual contexts and practices that encourage intentional actions, self-knowledge, and courageous engagement with life?

Why Spirituality?

SPIRITUALITY IS IMPORTANT because it is essential to good psychological health, especially in the second half of the life span. By the time we reach the age of thirty-five or forty, most of us begin to recognize our mortality if we haven't already confronted it through illness, accident, or loss. For

women the confrontation with aging also brings a painful challenge to the wish to be a lifelong desire-awakening maiden.
But if we have developed a spiritual purpose, we discover that
we can thrive through midlife and after in many ways that
were barely imaginable earlier. A sense of purpose that tran-
scends our personal identity (the feeling that "I'm useful and
have a bigger purpose than just promoting my identity") is rad-
ically important to self-esteem and self-determination as we
age. Such a conviction is a shield against the slings and arrows
of hag-bitch projections that follow from our claims to female
authority.

Without some spiritual context we face the future with
despair, inner emptiness, or restlessness. A religious or spiritual
orientation does not erase these negative experiences; they are
a part of human life. But such a perspective gives them meaning, makes them understandable in a way that sustains our
hope and interest in life. This is not a sleight of hand or mind.
Rather it is an essential root of human creativity and development: a mythology or Big Story through which we discover the
spiritual meaning of our individual lives.

The Big Story

THE BIG STORY is an account of what it means to be alive
and human, what is true and good, and why we should act as
we do. We regard our own lives as understandable only in the
context of some kind of Big Story, our basis for "reality." We
need a Big Story in order to make sense of what goes on within
and around us, but not all Big Stories offer possibilities for spiritual development.

In our era we implicitly accept a form of scientific realism as
part of the Big Story. Most of us do not understand how elec-

tricity works, for instance, but we use electric appliances with
the belief that this technology stems from a scientific set of
principles (the Big Story) that are predictable and control-
lable. Countless times each day we believe in the Big Story of
science when we accept on faith the effectiveness of medi-
cines, the operation of computers, the explanations of genetics—without any real understanding of them. But the Big
Story of science provides little guidance for our personal spiritual development; we would be hard-pressed to find a symbolic
connection to it that would help us know what our purpose in
life is.

Both Carl Jung and psychiatrist Robert Jay Lifton have
written about the importance of a "symbolic connection"
between our individual lives and a spiritual context that provides meaning. If, for example, you believed that the sun rose
over the horizon every morning because you performed a certain ritual, then you would be fulfilling a great task every morning. To give a contemporary example, if you have faith that
your efforts to heal conflicts and respect others will increase
possibilities for world peace, then those actions take on signifi-
cance beyond your personal concerns. By contrast, if all your
activities and desires seem meaningless in the larger world—
random or disconnected from everything else—then your individual life is trivial. When the symbolic connection is broken,
we feel numb and aimless, or we search for substitutes for some
meaning beyond our personal concerns.

I agree with Jung and Lifton, who claim that the symbolic
connection is broken for many people in our era because we
have no unifying Big Story that allows us to see our individual
purpose in a spiritual context. But we still have the need for
it, so we develop leisure activities that are life-threatening
(such as bungee jumping and skydiving), invest ourselves in

beliefs in alien worlds, or seek altered states through drugs. These substitute for spiritual meaning by providing experiences that break down our ordinary sense of self and connect us with awe or mystery (loosely congruent with science). Yet none of these pastimes can offer reliable spiritual meanings that evolve over time.

Without some kind of transcendent meaning, we cannot live fully because the constraints and suffering of human life are too severe. We need to find a way to make our pain and misery tolerable, even beneficial. Among the stories available some people embrace our contemporary scientific adventure as the Big Story of progress, miracles, predictions, and salvation that will defeat human adversity in the future. Others embrace the adventure of personal development through investigating, studying, and meditating on subjective life. Through practices of self-awareness and self-knowledge, these people discover both the patterns and the transcendence of self via relationship and interconnectedness. Others turn to more traditional spiritual adventures and make use of religious teachings and institutional offerings of Big Stories that may conflict with science but provide greater spiritual guidance. Still others become involved with a humanitarian cause and put their spiritual energies into developing a future that improves survival for the poor and disadvantaged, and/or protects the environment for all of us.

The Great Quest(ion)s

IF WE DEVELOP into emotionally mature adults, we have to give up fantasies that once sustained us—such as, There are perfect people in the world with absolute control of their lives, and I will become one of them. Stripped of childish illusions of power and control, we are left to face the underlying insecurities of being human: nothing is permanent; everyone ages and dies; everyone is vulnerable; there are no guarantees that if I behave well only good things will happen to me. Spiritual questions naturally arise from this confrontation, and they must be encountered seriously if we are to live life to the fullest. Why am I here? What does it mean to be human? What happens when I die? Our attempts to answer lead to the discovery of our spiritual desires.

In Chapter Four I talked about Marjorie, the hothouse mother consumed with her hidden desire to make her son Henry into a Divine Child who could supply her with all that she felt she lacked. He would be a charming, successful genius who reflected her mothering. Over the course of her therapy Marjorie encountered her feelings about mothering more honestly. She discovered her ambivalence, and she found that she could discipline Henry more effectively by recognizing that he was both good and bad, not simply *wonderful*. Once she allowed Henry greater freedom to feel his ambivalence about her, Marjorie was freed from her illusions about motherhood. No longer did she believe that she had been created to be a perfect mother to Henry. Instead, she started to wonder about her larger purpose in life.

At the age of forty Marjorie was beginning to feel a shortness to the years ahead. She noted aches and pains in her body and often remarked that she wasn't going to live forever. Although she longed for a transformative spiritual meaning, she felt obliged to take her children to the same uninspiring Protestant church in which she had grown up. Her husband had no objections to this form of religious education for the children, but he rarely participated in the services. Marjorie said she was "bored to tears" in this church, yet she did not feel free to join something else.

Like so many of her friends, Marjorie had a variety of New Age beliefs—in astrology, past lives, sometimes even alien abductions. She told me she didn't want to "close the door on something prematurely," and she found many of these ideas fascinating. Instead of using her energy to face the spiritual question What's my purpose in life? she voraciously read accounts of past lives, watched *The X-Files* religiously, and frequented a nearby psychic for predictions of her future and readings of her astrological chart or other oracles. It was difficult for me to challenge Marjorie's beliefs in these endeavors because they were part of her spiritual identity, but they were only substitutes for a symbolic connection to a life of meaning.

While we were interpreting one of Marjorie's dreams, some tension arose between us about the idea of spirituality. I suggested that spirituality had to connect in some realistic way with everyday life in order to be vital and engaging. Marjorie disagreed with me, saying that her spirituality was "on another plane" and provided insights that were beyond her ordinary life.

From this confrontation we looked at the way Marjorie's parental complexes seemed similar to her spirituality and discovered that she compensated for flaws and limitations in her parents' ability to care for her as an infant and child with illusions about their strengths. She had developed partly fictionalized stories about them so that she could feel proud they were her parents. Rather than acknowledging her mother's emotional withdrawal and depression, Marjorie imagined that her mother was truly kind and sensitive. She explained away her father's temper and unpredictable demands by believing that he was fundamentally generous and lively, just occasionally overwhelmed by his duties. These were not wholly false images, but they were romanticized, filled out by Marjorie's imagination of what good parents should be.

Thus her first encounter with transcendent meaning—her relationship with her parents—had required a fictional account of what was taking place, and her adult spiritual development continued this fiction. Marjorie went to a church where she was not deeply affected, tried to fit in, then looked for something soothing or mysterious in her New Age beliefs, even though they did not really satisfy her spiritual yearning.

When Marjorie saw how her psychological complexes interfered with her spiritual development, she began to look more deeply at her own desires. She had wanted a spiritual orientation that would excite her, that would emphasize the grandeur rather than the suffering of life. In the absence of a Big Story that could supply authentic symbolic connection with her everyday life, Marjorie had plugged into the sci-fi, New Age mentality of the media and some of her friends. Largely this was a distraction from her more personal spiritual questions. Now she was ready to find the answers to her own questions: what did she want to do with her life, and what could she do for herself and her children to find spiritual nourishment that felt authentic and truthful?

Must We Be Good?

FOR CENTURIES, INSTITUTIONAL religions have expected women to be ignorant, passive, receptive, devout, silent, and selfless. In reaction many women have turned away from all types of organized religions. But to fully engage with our spiritual yearnings and to develop them actively in a way that supports everyday life, we (people, in general) typically must join some group or community that has similar beliefs. Without a community we cannot see ourselves easily and we are always vulnerable to our psychological complexes—even when we have developed insight and understanding. Other people, with similar spiritual desires and beliefs, can help us to stay honest, stick to the path, and recognize the signposts of where we are. A community adds a level of support and emotional engagement that can be the essence of spiritual development. But in order for a community to support spiritual development, it needs to suit you well *and* you need to engage with that community—not simply wait for it to affect you.

There now are many alternatives available for women who want to be self-determining Subjects, actively involved in discovering and understanding their own spiritual development within a community of like-minded people. But these endeavors are challenging and often confusing because patriarchy has shaped our religious and spiritual symbols for many centuries. Images of women in patriarchal religions have traditionally discouraged female sovereignty.

If we engage with a religious or spiritual community, must we fit into traditional feminine roles to be accepted and supported? If we don't fit into the roles, perhaps we shouldn't be in the communities. And perhaps even more insidious is an almost palpable fear that once again we will simply have to be "good"—good girls, good mothers, good wives—in order to have any part in spirituality. Women agonize over a single question—Am I too selfish?—struggling with the belief that focusing on ourselves is selfish when it comes to spiritual or religious issues. We've been taught that we're inferior to men in our ability to be pure-hearted and wise. We've been described as more narcissistic, childish, unclean, and passive than men—even though we may be parenthetically extolled for being nurturant and motherly. The roles of maiden, muse, mother, and wife (emphasized for women in all traditional religions) have assumed that we should be selfless or that we have no self or soul—that is, no capacity for spiritual development. Even when the role of female celibate or monastic is permitted, women are still considered inferior to men in their spiritual capacities because of the nature of being female.

Selfish or Selfless: The Wrong Question

ADDING TO THE CONFUSION surrounding religion and female self-determination is the fact that many contemporary and traditional religious and spiritual teachings, especially those involving meditational practices, focus on letting go of the individual self. Psychiatrist Mark Epstein, writing about Buddhist teachings, says:

> The Western psychological notion of what it means to have a self is flawed. . . . Self-development, self-esteem, self-confidence, self-expression, self-awareness, and self-control are our most sought after attributes. But Buddhism teaches us that happiness does not come from any kind of acquisitiveness, be it material or psychological. Happiness comes from letting go.

Many women will read this passage and believe that they should let go of developing self-determination, self-awareness, and self-control without realizing that what is implied here is an *attitude about* the self, not the *functioning of* the self.

Women are easily misled by language that assumes we have mastered the art of personal sovereignty. At the heart of many religious and spiritual teachings is the assumption that human beings have sovereignty over their own lives, with no acknowledgment of how this may be compromised for women. Central to the moral and ethical codes of all the great world religions is the belief that human beings have free will, choice, intentions of their own. When they act on these intentions, they create consequences for themselves and others. All religions instruct us to pay close attention to our intentions and actions if we are to be ethical and moral.

In English we imbue the very word *self* with intentionality. This means that self-development, self-awareness, and self-determination are connected to living an intentional life, being responsible for ourselves and our subjective responses. But in patriarchal cultures and religions, women have been uniformly discouraged in all the self-aspects that are named in Epstein's passage, and this certainly has not led to their spiritual enlightenment. Without the knowledge and development of self-determination, women do not understand what it means to have free will. Women have not been free, or have not felt free, to live responsibly by the choices they make. As we have seen throughout the book, this situation has created conditions that reinforce the false promises of living as Objects of Desire.

When women look to others—masters, psychics, astrologers, gurus, leaders, or priests—to instruct them in answers to questions that they have not asked, they are at risk for spiritual abuse: a situation in which a woman is used as an Object of Desire by someone who is supposed to be on a higher spiritual level. Sexual, emotional, or financial abuse by a spiritual leader becomes spiritual abuse when the experience is justified or rationalized through a so-called spiritual practice.

Feminist therapist and theorist Demaris Wehr writes that

spiritual abuse is especially harmful because it takes place in an environment that is seen as sacred. The spiritual seeker "tends to be more accepting, more trusting, and less skeptical than he or she might be in a secular setting." Spiritual abuse often occurs in a situation in which there is some alteration of consciousness, renewed energy, miracle of healing, or the promise of such. The consequences of betrayal are extensive because trust has been broken not only in relation to a particular setting or individual but often in relation to a whole set of values and beliefs, even perhaps to the ability to trust spiritually again.

Spiritual yearnings then become tainted, and development is derailed through the mix of cynicism, doubt, fear, and hurt that is bred by the unsavory combination of a desire for power and the seeker's spiritual longings. The desire for power originates in the corrupt leader but is reinforced by a recipient who is confused, overwhelmed, ignorant about her self-determination, her rights to personal sovereignty.

One aspect of healing from abuse recommended by Wehr is to redefine the sacred, "to move God from an external to an internal authority. . . . God didn't really sanction any abuse, even though the abuse was done in the name of the Holy. What *really* is Sacred, Holy, God? What does your deepest sense of who you are, your deepest integrity, demand of you?" What is lost or buried in spiritual abuse is the seeker's ability to make her own decisions. Mixing betrayal and spirituality, power and love, abuse blurs the longings for wisdom or transcendence with the sense that one must give one's self away.

In order to be spiritually and psychologically mature, we have to take responsibility for ourselves, to be accountable for our thoughts, intentions, actions. When we are driven by our complexes or jettison our desires by projecting them onto others—wanting to be the Objects of Desire—then we are not living consciously by our intentions. To know our own intentions and desires we must gain a knowledge of our complexes. We can partly answer the question Who am I? in learning how we specifically create suffering in ourselves and others. Recognizing how we create it, we can recognize how to stop it. We then have a choice rather than a compulsion.

Expanding, Not Giving Away the Self

So WHAT ABOUT letting go of the self? Instead of the language of letting go, I have found it useful to think of expanding or sharing the self to include all that we sense and feel in our connection to others. If we expand the self, then we don't have to give it away. Instead, we come to recognize that such spiritual teachings point to the fact that we are never separate from anything else in this universe; our fundamental condition is interdependence. Many women understand this almost intuitively if they have extended themselves into their children—which feels as though they have multiple locations of self. Using the metaphor of expanding, we get around the thorny questions of whether we have to "be somebody" before we can "be nobody." For women at this time in history, it seems that the dualism of somebody-nobody is misleading, and often dangerous.

We women need to be especially clear about self-determination, about being Subjects of our own desires, while recognizing that the self is a function and not a thing. We should also become alert to our self-conscious emotions (pride, envy, shame, jealousy, guilt, embarrassment, self-pity) that preoccupy us with worry about our images. We can struggle to let go of these emotions and turn ourselves more directly to tasks at hand.

Throughout this book I have recommended not being good and nice but instead being sincere, compassionate, alert to the choices you make. My feelings about spirituality are expressed in the images and meanings of Mary Oliver's evocative poem "Wild Geese." She reminds us that we do not have to be contained, penitent, or self-effacing to engage the spiritual aspects of our existence. We need only dive wholeheartedly into the excitement and energy of our own physical and emotional being, especially through our connection with the natural world around us.

No matter your circumstances, fears, loneliness—even your confusion—she says, "the world offers itself to your imagination/calls to you like the wild geese, harsh and exciting. . . ." Spiritual longings and questions arise in this kind of immediate and authentic encounter.

Engaging Your Quest(ion)s

WHEN IT COMES TO the questions of why we are here, what it means to be human, and why we die, we must go beyond the province of psychology. To confront these questions, we turn to a Big Story that offers a spiritual context for our development.

In my own life, I find the Big Story of compassion useful for stepping out of self-consciousness, restlessness, and hopelessness. *Compassion*, in English, literally means "suffering with." The word points to the possibility of empathy, or feeling another's pain or difficulty. Compassion stirs our natural altruism, our desire to help. Anytime I have truly helped another person or animal, I have been rewarded many times over and

above the effort. Developing the capacity to give effective
help, to enter into another's unique situation and see what is
useful and what is not, has expanded my self-knowledge, not in
a personal way but in the way of understanding what it means
to be human.

I have learned that my self is enhanced by every compassionate act, and indeed that I cannot make the distinction
between self and other at these moments because there is no
distinction: there is one action that encompasses both people—or all who are involved. My practice of Buddhist meditation has assisted me in being keenly aware of sharing self in
this way, relaxing in my sense of self without excessive self-
consciousness and self-protection.

The peace activist Joanna Macy describes her approach to
compassionate action in a way that resonates with mine: "Even
my pain for the world is a function of this mutual belonging
like a cell experiencing the larger body. Because it shows that
causality, or power, resides in relationships rather than in per-
sons or institutions, it offers the courage to resist conformity
and to act in new ways to change the situation." Resisting
conformity here does not mean rebelling but rather being alert
to the choices we make, the implications of our actions.
Responding usefully to others' pain and suffering, knowing we
can make choices that change the world, keeps our focus large
and encompassing rather than small and fearful.

But this is just one way to answer the question of how to
expand the self through spiritual inquiry. My client Marjorie,
in seeking a sense of bigger purpose in her life, began to attend
a women's group at her church and to read some books about
women's spirituality, especially by the feminist Starhawk. She
found these books helpful in a more practical way than her earlier New Age reading.

Influenced by her women's group, her reading, and her therapy, Marjorie began to study yoga and meditation. In the long
run these interests led her to open a little shop that specialized
in alternative approaches to women's health—offering yoga,
vitamin supplements, aromatherapy products, and other
health and cosmetic products. In this work she integrated her
business skills, her ability to organize people, and her spiritual
interests.

When Marjorie left psychotherapy, she had changed her
religious affiliation and was attending Quaker meetings with
her children and husband. Participating in a feminist group in
her Quaker community, she had also begun to study advanced
yoga so that she could become a teacher. Her spirituality had
matured to the point that she felt symbolically connected to
the world around her, confident of the religious teachings she
was offering her children, and even hopeful amidst the appar-
ent chaos of our times.

Self-determining women engage their spiritual questions
directly and personally, and find ways to answer through traditional religions, feminist spirituality, or other contemporary
spiritual practices. Feminism has encouraged all of us to make
choices and to understand why and how we are doing things,
to know the implications of our actions for our humanity. From
a feminist perspective, women cannot thrive in any religious or
spiritual environment in which they simply follow rules that
were invented, at least in part, to keep men functioning as
Subjects and women as Objects. So we have to be watchful as
we engage with spiritual environments and practices to keep
our intentionality in the foreground if we are to have personal
sovereignty.

Jane, a client I see in psychotherapy, recently brought up a
dilemma she had encountered in her meditation practice. She

had been practicing a form of Zen Buddhist sitting meditation for several months. Her sitting is immobile, still without random movements of her body, even though her muscles might be strained or she might experience an itch or cough. She had been meditating long enough to learn that itches and coughs have a way of fading if you just "sit with them" and let them pass. Jane knew some of the benefits of holding still and not giving in to the impulse to move. She liked the effect of watching the "profile" of her need to react: the intensification of it, then its gradual fading and disappearance.

Yet Jane was often reminded of her early fundamentalist Christian background, which had demanded that she endure pain in silence and suppress pleasure. She remembered being humiliated for being "weak" because she was a woman, and she worried that once again she was forcing herself to endure pain because it would teach her a lesson. From her psychotherapy she had learned a very different way of living, much more in line with the Mary Oliver poem: expecting the richness and harshness of the world to call her forth in a way she could trust. Now she worried that through her spiritual practice she was forcing herself into an old pattern of self-abnegation.

My response was to ask her what she wanted. She had already experienced some benefit in seeing the rise and fall of her subjective reactions, and she had learned enough about her practice to know what the long-term benefits could be. But I stressed the fact that she was the only one to decide whether or not the meditation "was worth it"—not in the sense of being worth her time and energy but rather in the sense of affirming her experience without promoting too many negative, oppressive images of herself. Only she could answer this question.

Is It Worth It?

THE QUESTION Is it worth it? is one we all need to ask and answer if we are to become Subjects of our spiritual desires. This means an ongoing evaluation of where we stand in relation to rules and codes in our religious practices and traditions. Does this work for me as a woman? If not, can I work to change it? As the Buddhist scholar and feminist writer Rita Gross says, "Because patriarchal religions will not rid themselves of their patriarchy, a feminist who wishes to remain within that tradition must take nothing on faith and test everything."

All institutionalized religions—Judaism, Christianity, Islam, Hinduism, Buddhism—contain practices and rules that are oppressive to women. Influenced by feminism and female leadership, these institutions are changing, even though the process of change is slow and the traditions are strong. For any woman, then, the question will be whether she can keep her sanity, her connections with others, and her belief in her own sovereignty in the face of the time and effort it might take to participate in a patriarchal religion, even one that is in the process of feminist transformation.

Many of us are still confused about how to be Subjects of spiritual desires without miring ourselves in power struggles or isolating ourselves in yet another way from other women. My client Anne says, "I have so many things to be grateful for, and I want to return what has been given to me through some kind of spiritual expression. I want an outlet or a group, but I hesitate to get involved with anything religious in an *institutional* sense because everything gets so complicated." She feels conflict when she goes to a formal mass at her Episcopal church, a tradition that she has known since childhood. Even though one of the pastors at her church is a woman, and even though a female bishop presides in a nearby diocese, Anne feels that her church still operates according to the same male-oriented principles it did when she was a child. Women priests may lead in a more relational style, but their presence has not affected much of the decision making at higher levels, even in her own church. Anne enjoys the ceremony, but she fears that she justifies her involvement because she can't motivate herself to do something else. She is as uncertain about looking further into her religion as she is ambivalent about looking for another one. If she leaves her tradition she cuts herself off from her family functions, but if she stays she has to be willing to challenge the status quo in order to even open the door to some major changes she would like to see.

I, too, question the patriarchal roots of my religion. I became a formal practitioner of Buddhism in 1970, before I became a feminist and a mother. Even then I recognized that Buddhism, especially Zen, would become my mainstay for being clearheaded and happy. But from the beginning I sometimes felt a wordless fear and a rising anger about practices and rules that were imposed on me without my understanding them. I had no idea how to verbalize that conflict, and I didn't.

After only four years, having learned so much that was tremendously important to me, I realized that I was experiencing the same kind of shame and humiliation, negative feelings about myself and my goodness, that I had felt in my childhood religion. I was confused, sometimes even terrified, that I was once again in a "fear-based" religion. I was troubled by the severity of Zen practices that seemed to lack a human touch, and I did not know why practitioners had to be so subdued and isolated. So, without much forethought and almost to my own surprise, I left the Zen center I had joined. When I spoke to my teacher about wanting to leave, he responded kindly, in a way that allowed me to continue to identify with being a Buddhist.

For almost twenty years I practiced on my own, sometimes using formal Zen methods and sometimes not, often associating with various Quaker groups as a means of being in community with like-minded people. I read a lot about the history of Buddhism and gained knowledge that made my practice more understandable, gave it a larger context. Identifying myself as "a Buddhist," I felt sheepish about not having a group affiliation, but I also believed that my intuition was correct about needing to be on my own for a time. Then in 1993, after seeking a new teacher in a number of places, I was reunited with my first teacher and the American Zen center where I began.

In the ensuing time feminism and women had influenced Buddhism and the center where I had practiced. Now I find there is room to ask questions, to express doubts and problems, and to raise issues that might conflict with the mainstream opinion. I am grateful to have returned to my community and to have so many friends and so much history there. I am also aware I still feel nagging doubts about the severity of some of the practices and rules that have been imported from Japanese society. As I have become better acquainted with Japanese history and culture, I have realized that Zen has been influenced by many (sometimes hidden) beliefs that are oppressive to women— arising especially from the hierarchical traditions of Confucianism in China and Japan. So I continue to examine and question while I engage with my practice and Zen community.

If God Is Male

AS I TRACE my own spiritual history, I cannot imagine that I would be participating in a Zen Buddhist community today were it not for American feminism. Buddhism is a nontheistic religion (it does not deny the existence of supernatural beings but has no Absolute or Supreme Being who can confer salvation or damnation), so it has no gendered Absolute, no God. Thus in the 1970s, feeling secure in Buddhism, I did not give much thought to God or gods of any sort until I began to read feminist theology.

A 1979 collection of essays called *Womanspirit Rising: A Feminist Reader in Religion*, edited by Carol Christ and Judith Plaskow, introduced me to a broad range of new developments from feminist theology. These essays awoke me to the idea that a male god image affected our entire society, not only our Judeo-Christian religions, but in the ways we looked at everything, all of our values and all of our environments. Six years earlier the theologian Mary Daly had said, "If God is male, then male is God." Spoken clearly and boldly, Daly's words were for many the clarion call to look at the political components of traditional religions.

This perspective revealed my experiences at the Zen center in a new light. I had found a language for my silent conflicts. Even in that nontheistic environment there was a clear implication that "male is God" because all the teachers, leaders, role models were male—and their authority was unquestioned.

Today women can be found in positions of authority and influence in Buddhism and other major religions in our society, but we are only at the point of departure in having an effect on many traditions. Struggling for leadership, changing language and forms of thinking, we continually renew our desires to make our religions responsive and compassionate to the needs of all kinds of people. Back in 1979 Christ and Plaskow believed that feminism would "present a growing threat to patriarchal religion less by attacking it than by simply leaving it behind." Their words have not proven to be true. Although women-based religions have gained wide popularity, many women have stayed within the framework of institutional religion while recognizing it as an instrument of their betrayal. Women clergy, religious teachers, and monastics of all traditions have brought about remarkable, some almost unimaginable, changes by working from within their institutions.

Working within the Traditions

FEMINISM HAS THREATENED the religious status quo of many traditions by questioning and undercutting the foundations of the roles and beliefs that keep power in the ranks of the few. In their efforts to disrupt the damaging effects of elevating some and oppressing others, feminist religious leaders and theologians are interested in much more than putting women into leadership positions in religious institutions. They are interested in reconceptualizing faith so that all people recognize that they are active shapers of their spiritual lives and not passive recipients.

Feminist influences on religions and spiritual practices are making an impact. In my view American feminism of the past twenty-five years has been more successful in theology and spiritual practices than in other areas of our society. Mainline seminaries and religious institutions are now virtually forced to include feminist works in their bibliographies and course offerings; even those who reject it must become acquainted with feminist theology as a matter of professionalism. We cannot say the same of professions such as medicine or law, or of government and business.

Feminist theologians and women priests, rabbis, pastors, and teachers have opened and strengthened new possibilities of greater participation for all people—but especially for women who have been denied the right—to be Subjects in a spiritual process. Feminism has challenged all of us to ask the questions we want to answer.

Yet the faith that it is possible to practice female self-determination in a traditional patriarchal religion is very much a work in progress. Psychotherapist and feminist Rachel Josefowitz Siegel describes herself as a "loud, proud Jewish mother, grandmother, great-grandmother" and has written numerous articles on issues of feminism and Judaism. Writing about changes that have allowed women to practice as rabbis, and girls and women to learn the sacred text, the Torah, Siegel says, "The institutional changes are far from universal and often have the quality of crazy-making illusions, being only superficial, while the basic attitudes and behaviors have hardly changed at all." Only since 1922 have Jewish girls been permitted to have a coming-of-age ceremony, called *bat mitzvah*, and still they are excluded from such a ritual in the Conservative and Orthodox sects of Judaism. This ceremony, available to boys for more than twenty-five hundred years, introduces a young person as an adult into the community of practitioners. Among other things preparation for the ceremony includes learning the scholarly language (Hebrew) in which the sacred books are written. Through most of the history of Judaism, girls and women were not permitted to learn this language, so they had no access to sacred texts.

Now that girls and women *can* be initiated into the domains of power from which they had been excluded for centuries, they are confronted with information about ritual and tradition that they often find unwelcome. After acquiring the knowledge of the Torah in the latter part of her adult life, Siegel was surprised at her ambivalence about what she had learned.

> As I learned more, I became aware of my aversion to the sexist, hierarchical, and vengeful messages that are embedded in Jewish texts. I began to ask myself whether this was what I really wanted to perpetuate. The question that emerged was whether it is possible to retain the positive elements of Jewish teachings, while reframing or rejecting the objectionable elements.

Siegel answered this question affirmatively and has been working for the inclusion of women in prayer, institutions, and communal leadership while challenging the status quo of texts. She has worked within her own community and through national organizations to open more possibilities for women to question and discuss sacred texts with their rabbis. She has called on her own granddaughters to discuss with them their developing identities as feminist Jewish women. She has insisted that traditional male hierarchy be challenged and that Jewish women recognize the important knowledge they bring to their community, knowledge based on their experiences of work and life. Through all of this Siegel accepts nothing from tradition without questioning its specific meaning for women.

The Catholic theologian Mary Hunt raises some of the same

concerns. Is it possible to eliminate what is objectionable, retain positive elements of Catholicism, and be a viable Catholic feminist? Hunt believes that it is, but only by focusing on changing structure, dogma, and language, and eliminating power hierarchies. Although she believes that the ordination of women as Roman Catholic priests is increasingly likely, she is dubious about its effects. Hunt, like many other Catholic feminists, feels ordination would be a hollow victory: "To ordain women into hierarchical structures and . . . demand that they be celibate and under the direct control of male bishops will be no great accomplishment." In fact, such an arrangement would shore up male power, reinforcing most of the oppressive aspects of Roman Catholicism and "leave untouched the many doctrinal and dogmatic issues which are so problematic."

Hunt stresses that women should not be confused by winning certain trappings in a patriarchal religion:

> The major change [through feminist influences on religion] is not in the gender of the divine, though female imagery and symbolism, as well as more abstract, nongendered notions are important. Rather it is the idea that women are not meant to be passive recipients of religion but active shapers. . . . This signals a fundamental change from a hierarchical model with religious professionals . . . in charge to women taking responsibility for our own religious lives.

In her memoir on being a Catholic feminist, *Ordinary Time*, writer Nancy Mairs provides an example of feminist Catholicism in her descriptions of her own spiritual community. All in her community are committed to social change, especially to working for peace and justice, and serving the hungry and homeless. Every other Sunday afternoon her community meets in informal gatherings in homes for a "leisurely Mass," discussion, and a potluck supper. This type of "house-church" is closer to the manner in which early Christianity was practiced.

Before Christians could worship publicly (when they were still persecuted by Romans), they met quietly in their homes to gather around a table and celebrate, discuss, reminisce, eat, and drink. Women played a major role in this movement, often being the central organizers. Women were priests, prophets, and probably even bishops during the first thousand years of church history. But during the third and fourth centuries, as Christianity entered the public sphere, conflict arose among Christians about female leadership. Men became the major leaders and demanded the same subjugation of women that prevailed in society. Church scholars from Origen to Augustine argued, not from theological but from social premises, to condemn female prophecy and leadership. Eventually the church adopted the position that women by their nature were not fit to teach or baptize because their place was in the home (as maidens, mothers, wives), not in the public domain.

Thus official female leadership was all but lost for hundreds of years within Christian churches. In 1853 the first ordination of a female minister was performed by the United Church of Christ (UCC). Other denominations eventually followed; now over 20 percent of UCC ministers are female. In 1973 the first female priest was ordained in the Episcopal Church, and today there are more than 1,950 female priests in the Episcopal Church, and 2.3 percent of bishops are female. Yet across all categories of ordained ministers and priests, women have considerably less power than men in comparable roles, in terms of their status, decision making, and numbers of practitioners they oversee.

In contrast with Christianity, there is no record of early female leadership in Judaism. Ignorance of the sacred language and texts was imposed on women through most of the formal history of the religion, in the belief that it was women's role to be supportive of Jewish traditions through domestic and nurturant practices but not knowledgeable of the core teachings. The combination of internalized inferiority and oppression from the non-Jewish world and learned ignorance from within Judaism leaves even feminists feeling "ambivalent about acting, speaking, or being Jewish."

But in spite of these negative internal and external discouragements, Jewish women are actively making their voices and concerns heard. In 1972 the first woman rabbi was ordained in the Jewish Reform Movement, and within a decade women constituted more than a third of the students at the Reform seminary. Feminist Jewish study and Rosh Chodesh groups are flourishing in both Reform and Conservative congregations, introducing new areas of Jewish study that focus on women at international, national, and regional conferences. The major task of Jewish feminism at this time is confirming women's knowledge and ability to speak out about their Jewishness, questioning and claiming what they know, searching for an authentic Jewishness that is not limited to male-dominated labels and ideas.

Buddhism, like Christianity, has at its roots a belief in the fundamental equality of the sexes. The ancient texts that preserve the stories of the Buddha's life also preserve the early stories of women monastics who achieved the highest goals of a spiritual life as formulated by earliest Buddhism. Buddhism is unique among world religions in having these female "songs of triumph," as Rita Gross calls them, scriptural accounts of women's experiences of enlightenment recorded in the sixth century B.C.E.

Even with such events on record, though, Buddhism gradually subordinated and oppressed women, assuming their fundamental spiritual inferiority to men. Throughout its twenty-five-hundred-year history, and until the advent of Western Buddhism about forty years ago, many Buddhists "believed that women needed to be reborn as men before they could attain enlightenment." Although this belief is now widely thought to be wrong, it is still held by some more traditional Buddhists.

All the same, feminist women—like myself—are attracted to Buddhism and to Buddhist meditational practices because they are grounded in experience. Like feminism, Buddhism presumes that we are blinded to our true nature by ignorance of how things are. Both practices encourage us to break down and release the obsessions and illusions that hide from us the true beauty and contentment of our lives. Feminist women may see Buddhist practices as ways to augment their own processes of self-discovery and activism, offering well-tested methods for awakening to the fullness of the present moment.

Yet when one reads Buddhist scriptures and teachings, or the Western scholarship of Buddhism, even most of the instructional books written for the beginning meditator, one finds few references to women's experiences, especially in ways that might be different from men's. Consequently, until very recently there has been little to no instruction about using formal meditation practice to improve and enhance the experience of relationships, childbirth, or parenting. Even though daily physical work—cleaning, gardening, cooking, building—

is a major part of Zen training, it is rarely compared specifically with managing a household and caring for a family. Contemporary feminist Buddhists are filling this gap by integrating women's everyday lives into Buddhist practices and by developing a literature and approach that can sustain the feminist gaze alongside the meditative gaze.

In this section, I have offered only a glimpse into the sexism and oppression in a few religions, and what women are doing to make changes. Because feminists have continued to practice within the confines of patriarchal religions, and because these religions offer long and well-tested traditions of spiritual development, we can to varying degrees become Subjects of our spiritual desires within them. Repeatedly feminists stress the critical importance of taking nothing on blind faith, following no rules or codes without understanding them, then deciding what can be used to develop integrity, wisdom, and transcendence in a way that supports self-determination.

Working outside Traditions

WHAT, THEN, OF THE RELIGIONS that step outside patriarchy? Alternatives to traditional religions in New Age, Goddess, and Neo-Pagan groups have been established and organized by women—some of them explicitly along the lines of feminist concerns. They welcome and encourage self-determination and are sensitive to the internalized inferiority that has developed in many women through traditional religious practices.

Since the 1979 publication of Drawing Down the Moon by Margot Adler, the Neo-Pagan movement has been one of the fastest-growing forms of spirituality in the United States, with estimates of more than 200,000 members. Neo-Paganism is a loose affiliation of several forms of Goddess-based spirituality that are known collectively as Wicca, Witchcraft, or simply the Craft. There is no formal body of doctrine shared by all practitioners of the Craft, but most contemporary Wiccans use a system of practices that includes observance and celebration of certain festival days (such as the vernal equinox, the summer solstice, and other season-linked days) for worship of the Goddess and some Gods. Basic methods include the Sacred Circle, a meditative frame of mind, and tools such as a ritual knife (charged with certain energies) and quartz crystal.

Wiccan communities are composed of both women and men—with the exception of Dianic Wicca, which is women only—and are supportive of a wide variety of lifestyles and identities. Feminist groups include in their goals the ongoing creation and magic of women-oriented mysteries, such as changes in the female life cycle.

The Goddess is often visualized in three aspects that correspond with phases of the moon and with the female life cycle: Maiden, Mother, and Crone. Each of these aspects is described and imagined in ways that contradict patriarchal assumptions about them and increase women's strengths and abilities.

In ritual gatherings and study groups, women practitioners find that feminist concerns and spiritual longings can merge. In an atmosphere that is intended to be healing, women report a renewal of trust, recovering from psychological, physical, sexual, and spiritual abuse. Enlivened by their work together, spiritual feminists often champion social change. They share the belief that the "feminine principle" (connected to the Goddess, nature, nuturance, and growth) can contribute to a new synthesis of environmental, social, and gender healing.

Most practitioners find much to embrace in women-centered spirituality, although criticisms sometimes arise in regard to the exclusion of men, or sexism, in some Neo-Pagan groups. Wrestling with the forms and meanings of women living in patriarchy—while excluding men and focusing on the feminine life cycle—may not always be suited to the broader goals of women's self-determination. After all, most of us live in a society that includes male dominance, patriarchy, and men.

To succeed in this society while changing it often means reaching beyond Goddess images and emulating what seems to be workable, honest, and useful from role models of both sexes. Feminist spirituality appears to be single-mindedly devoted to images that enhance the power of the Goddess, that focus on the female reproductive cycle and its counterparts in the natural world. Furthermore, these Neo-Pagan groups are only about twenty-five years old at most. Their newness and uniqueness can mean that they do not fit easily with other aspects of women's lives—their families, friends, work settings. And sometimes their newness means long and arduous investments in working out even basic premises for how to function as a group.

Yet feminist spirituality has provided a much-needed alternative to patriarchal religions, as well as a clear message that spiritual life for women should be a matter of self-determination, self-esteem, and psychological health. The dialogue between feminists in patriarchal religions and those in women-created religions has strengthened and expanded the possibilities for women being Subjects of their spiritual desires, asking the questions they want to answer.

A Life of Meaning

EVEN WITH THE RISKS to women's self-determination in religious and spiritual settings, the benefits of spiritual devel-

opment outweigh the alternative of a wholly secular life. Without a spiritual context of some sort, life eventually seems too
overwhelming or depressing. It is the design of human life
itself—the long dependency of childhood, the fearful responsibility of adulthood, our aging, decline, and death—that motivates us to want something more than a personal identity and
material things.

Finding and engaging greater spiritual meaning can now be
a major component of an intentional life for anyone, even in
this scientific materialistic period. Feminists have significantly
improved things by emphasizing the relationship between
mature spirituality and emotional maturity, especially for
women. What feminism teaches about spiritual life is that we
are all responsible for developing it; it does not come from
somewhere on high.

I like the way Nancy Mairs expresses this idea from a Christian perspective: "We are not pitiful creatures huddled help-
lessly beneath a blizzard of miseries blown down by some
capricious power amusing himself at our expense. God is
with(in) each of us, and to the extent that we recognize and
honor God's presence in one another, we form and dwell in the
Community of God."

Finding the guidance of a tradition and the support of a
community to create and sustain spiritual meaning is now possible in a new way. Patriarchal religions (however reluctantly)
and feminist spirituality are joined in inviting us to be Subjects
of our spiritual desires.

SEVEN

The Paradox of Freedom and Desire

THROUGHOUT THIS BOOK I have talked about personal sovereignty in many contexts. As we've learned, personal sovereignty is different from assertiveness, individuality, independence, and getting your own way. Personal sovereignty or autonomy means feeling free to choose and to intend your actions. It requires practice and knowledge to make decisions in a way that is responsible, fulfilling, and satisfying. Expressing and supporting one's decisions with responsible action, ethical values, and clear language is a skill that can be developed only through conscious understanding and effort.

Cravings or longings that arise from desire for what was merely gratifying or pleasurable are not reliable guides to autonomy because they lead to impulse and addiction. We can never satisfy such cravings. They are based on the absence of something we want—slenderness, sex, money, even an ideal life partner—which no longer seems so exciting if or when we get it. Indeed, absence is the nature of such desire, experienced as emptiness, hunger, a lack, a yearning.

To be capable of personal sovereignty, you must come to *know* all of your desires. When you know your own desires, then you can choose among them—there is almost always more than one desire in a moment or a decision—and begin to discriminate the various paths your desires may lead you down. As you come to know the difference between your desire to be desirable and your desire to make your own decisions, you will understand more clearly how to cope with the pressures that arise in yourself and others when you begin to take yourself seriously. You will come to see that making claims for your own authority can sometimes lead to being seen as the hag-bitch, and you will learn how to conserve your authority in the face of challenges, attacks, and negative labels. Holding on to your authority means breathing deeply and standing firmly behind your decision without shame or blame.

Feminism has contributed to the development of women's sovereignty by opening many new avenues. New educational, athletic, relational, financial, professional, spiritual, religious, and lifestyle possibilities are available to all of us. Feminism has alerted us to the fact that gender identity and power are linked, and that it is vital to study and understand gender because gender is focal in a lot of what we think about human differences. Furthermore, feminism has shown us that gender is the product of social and environmental influences rather than biology and genetics.

What feminism has *not* clarified, though, is that certain types of power lead not to personal sovereignty but to black holes of despair, inner emptiness, and Hungry Ghost longings.

Girls and women have been encouraged, even supported by contemporary feminist and womanist groups, to go after what they want, to increase their power and self-esteem. But they are left unschooled in reading the signposts about what a particular power might mean. Consequently, many women believe that they *are* living out their own desires when they choose to be thin, chic, fashionable, sexy—imitating the anorectic muse of our era. And young mothers may feel that they have *chosen*, rather than been elected, to be full-time moms. But we have repeatedly seen that these are not free or autonomous choices when they develop from conscious or unconscious desires to be wanted, approved, worthy. The power of the Object of Desire is short-lived and never real. And even though younger women may not yet feel the depression and fear that are linked to being Objects of Desire, those of us who are beyond young adulthood know the burden of spending decades in beauty bondage or self-sacrifice, overwhelmed by others' needs, with no sense of control over our own lives. If we don't wake up to the problem of wanting to be wanted, and practice being the Subjects of our own desires, then we feel that others are always choosing for us, that our lives do not belong to us. We don't feel responsible for actions because we feel out of control.

An Intentional Life

WHAT DOES IT MEAN to feel "in control" of your life? The word *control* carries a lingering shadow for women because we are often called "controlling" by our husbands, boyfriends, and children. What I mean by *control* is the ability to make a choice. Personal sovereignty means that you choose from what is available in order to be intentional about your life. Even if you were locked in a prison cell, you could choose how to think about it. You could, through your own attitude, find a way to make use of your experience. Personal sovereignty is the ability to know and practice self-determination in whatever circumstances you find yourself. It depends on recognizing the boundaries and domain in which your autonomy exists, constantly seeing them clearly and extending them in favorable ways. When you feel in control of your life, you know yourself to be the author of your own actions and know that you always have choices.

Exercising choice and intentionality does not necessarily lead to the outcomes that we desire. No one is free to have her or his own way in human life. We are all limited by our weaknesses: mistakes, ignorance, circumstances, physical limitations, impermanence, illnesses, and death. Innumerable things fall completely outside our personal control every day. But as we learn how to make decisions in our daily lives, we become enlightened about our strengths and limitations, and how we depend on others for what we cannot do for ourselves.

In the early years of our development, we come into possession of the experience of being an individual self. That experience is hedged around by self-conscious emotions—envy, pride, shame, guilt, embarrassment, self-pity. These emotions encourage us to protect ourselves from others and convince us that the story of our world is "us against them." In order to break down those defenses and change the story to "us depending on them," we have to learn how to live intentionally. Coming to know the paradoxical nature of our autonomy—that we are always free to choose but limited in our knowledge and power—we come to be grateful for the people and situations that complete us, and we become more fully engaged with the choices that are available.

As we saw in the last chapter, free will or intentionality is at the heart of all the great religious and spiritual teachings. They teach that human beings are free to make their own choices and so are responsible for their actions in a way that animals are not. Here is how the Buddha said it, more than twenty-five hundred years ago:

> My actions are my only true belongings.
> I cannot escape the consequences
> of my actions.
> My actions are the ground
> on which I stand.

Social and political rights to sovereignty are vital to cultivating the experience of personal sovereignty. When people are not granted basic human rights—to life's resources, property, free expression, and suffrage—then it is difficult, sometimes even impossible, for them to develop their own feelings and experiences of personal sovereignty. The rights of women and minorities to vote and openly express their views, to hold positions of leadership, and to be originators of cultural and creative expressions are intrinsic to their experience of personal sovereignty. Women and minorities are relative newcomers to the domain of social and political freedom. We continue to be confused about our personal sovereignty, at least in part, because our expressions of power and authority are still not openly supported in many cultural, political, domestic, and relational arenas.

Thus, the knowledge and skill of developing autonomy are unfamiliar to many women. Those who identify with being Objects rather than Subjects function more in terms of what they "ought" to do, what they "have to" do, or what they "should" do because their sense of worth arises from others' evaluations, reflections, desires. They miss out on learning how to be self-determining, although they may believe that they have learned. The telltale sign that they are functioning more as Objects than as Subjects is, as we have repeatedly seen, feeling resentful and overwhelmed by their daily activities—feeling as though someone else were in charge.

The Hero Myth and Selfish Determination

MEN, ESPECIALLY WHITE MEN, have traditionally been shaped and schooled by society to be Subjects of their desires: they have been taught and shown by example how to be self-determining, to guide themselves by the belief that they must exercise their freedom in choosing a partner, a job, a direction, a political leader. This does not, however, mean that all men succeed in becoming Subjects of their own desires; they certainly do not.

Contemporary men are often confused about the nature of personal sovereignty because recently we have come to question and undermine the male myths that surround our sense of self. Traditionally, white men grew up believing that their autonomy was intimately related to their independence and individuality. In the United States our major cultural biases about the autonomous self have been cast in the form of the hero myth. This is the story of the lone genius, adventurer, athlete, artist, doctor, or scientist who triumphs against all odds to achieve a "unique" status because of his individual abilities. He is known as the Great Man, on whom we all depend for our meaning and miracles. Note that the myth never includes all the people on whom the great man depends for ideas, conversation, personal support, and services.

More important, this myth is a distortion of what it means

to be a Subject. The myth emphasizes individuality, aloneness, uniqueness, and independence to the exclusion of relationship, community, shared identity, and mature dependence. It confuses independence with autonomy. Men have been cheated out of a range of feelings and experiences in emulating the lone hero, resulting in unhealthy internal pressures, excessive narcissism, and feelings of isolation, resentment, and depression.

Fewer and fewer men feel good about following the hero myth as a personal life story. Yet the myth persists in our culture, causing many of us discomfort and confusion about our autonomous needs. Both women and men have questioned me when I say that self-determination is at the heart of feeling human. They unconsciously hear the phrase as "selfish determination." Should I put my needs *above* others'? Is it fair to be selfish and go after just what I want? are the questions they most often ask.

These are the wrong questions. They come from the assumption that your needs are intrinsically opposed to others' needs. They eliminate the idea that you can willingly *choose* to fulfill someone else's needs and wants when it is a matter of personal intention and not pressure from another. These questions obscure the real meaning of self-determination, as the freedom to choose, by surrounding it with anxiety about independence or individuality. They also eliminate the knowledge that choosing to help another can *increase* your own satisfaction and welfare, not simply because you were compassionate but because you *chose* to help when you could have chosen something else.

The right question—What do I want here?—needs to be posed with the understanding that your desires, needs, and wants can never be met perfectly, yet you are free to choose.

As I have said, I believe that we live in a world of dependence—with mature dependence as a worthy goal of adult development—so I also believe that everyone has needs for good, healthy relationships and desires to be of use to society and family. These considerations will always count heavily in our decision making, weighing one possibility against another, until we reach a viable direction. However, as we have seen again and again, if we give away personal sovereignty—either consciously or unconsciously—then we cannot be vitally engaged with our lives.

Living without Resentment

PERHAPS YOU RECALL Marla, from Chapter Three, who was married to Jack. Marla no longer believed that she could be an Object of Desire because her thighs were too flabby and her mouth had too many wrinkles around it. Believing that she could not stir the sexual excitement of her husband (or another man), she gave up wanting sex. When Marla came into psychotherapy she felt "liberated" because she could say No to sex with Jack. As we learned, though, her No was not a real choice because she could never say Yes. And her No was filled with resentment because, as she said, she felt constant guilt about it.

Unless you have two options, you don't have a choice, and Marla had only one option. She was not free. Marla began to say No to sex because she knew that she didn't want it. Her reason for not wanting it, though, was that she could no longer identify with being the desire-awakening maiden. Once she had been trapped as the muse, but now she was trapped as the hag.

The hag must get out of the woods of shame in order to become the Subject of her own desire. Marla came to psychotherapy to do that. Her hag identity had to transform into the belief that she could become an active sexual partner. For Marla, this meant letting go of her obsessions about appearance and engaging in physical pleasures more often with Jack. At first they massaged each other and spent some leisurely hours in bed together. Then Marla began to explore a few sexual pleasures—being stroked and kissed—and eventually found that, when she was relaxed, she could easily come to orgasm with Jack manually stimulating her. Having discovered this, Marla wanted to pursue her sexual responses further, in an atmosphere of respect for both herself and Jack.

But there were limitations. She and Jack had a two-year-old daughter and a five-year-old son, and Marla had a career as an elementary school teacher. There were physical limitations, too. Marla often had severe premenstrual syndrome (PMS) and could barely manage her moods during several days of each month. She had to make choices: how and how often could she get child care so that she and Jack could spend some leisurely, intimate time together? How could she manage her PMS so that her potential sexual engagements could take place during more than two weeks every month? At first she tended to fall back into her hag complex: it's no use, I was never meant to have sexual pleasures, I'm just not that kind of woman. But when she saw how resentful and bitter she became, with the knowledge now that she could be otherwise, Marla wanted greater freedom. She began to want both Yes and No as options for her sex life.

Eventually Marla was able to achieve a compromise: she could schedule certain Saturday mornings with Jack as "time for sexual pleasure" and plan to have the children stay with her

mom. She had to relinquish the idea of "spontaneous sex"—
something that she had always hoped would be a part of her
married life. If she was feeling physically exhausted, she and
Jack might agree to exchange orgasms manually rather than
have intercourse. Sometimes they would exchange massages if
orgasm seemed too burdensome. She had to give up the idea
that she had to feel physically good before she could be intimate with Jack.

Marla surprised herself with her ease of orgasm when there
was no pressure on her to be "seductive or beautiful." She said
that she felt "okay" about her body, and she knew that Jack
accepted her completely. Her sex life wasn't perfectly passionate, but it certainly brought her pleasure in a way it never had
before. The most important thing was that Marla felt free to
continue to explore and develop her sexuality; she was the
Subject of her own sexual desires. No longer was she resentful
and bitter, because she knew that she had choices and that
Jack did not control her sexuality.

Marla was able to decide in favor of creating a sex life and
changing her attitude about marital sex. But some decisions
are not that easy.

No Right Answers

DECIDING WHETHER OR NOT to have a child, for example,
often seems especially difficult. Single and married women—
lesbian and straight or bisexual—seek the "right" answers in
deciding whether or not to procreate. I have sat for weeks,
months, and even years in weekly psychotherapy sessions with
women who were trying to make this decision, which would
affect the remainder of their lives.

Are my personality and life situation suited to being a

mother? Is this the right time, or should I wait, even though the biological clock is ticking? Would it be better to undergo fertility techniques or to adopt? Should I have a committed partner as a condition for becoming a mother, even though waiting for one may mean that I am too old to get pregnant without technical assistance? What if I want a baby and my partner doesn't? With all kinds of options available to women who are privileged enough to use them, the questions are endless about how, when, and even what (girl or boy) to have.

It is my job to listen and explore all the options with my clients. What I see in the process, and what my clients come to see, is their secret desire to have guarantees, to know that what they have chosen is the "best" choice available. We women are fundamentally unpracticed in being the Subjects of our desires, so we are continuously wary about deciding what we want because we fear the consequences of that decision. It's not at all wrong to gather information and explore all options; gathering facts and hearing about others' experiences are necessary ingredients of making major life decisions. Eventually, though, a decision is just a decision. We will not know whether it was the right one or the wrong one until we live out its consequences (and perhaps we won't know then). But we will learn more about being Subjects of our desires and about being human.

Trying too hard to avoid negative consequences will throw us off course, because a decision means choosing from at least two options, not always making the best or the right choice but being willing to learn from choices. Making life decisions, and making everyday choices, means learning about risk and challenges. Our choices are never flawless. We are not gods; we cannot see the future; we cannot know all our effects on the interdependent world in which we live, the webs of relationships that sustain us. Yet we must choose, because if we do not we cannot be free. If we do not choose consciously, we will react unconsciously through our impulses and hidden desires, projecting our power needs and other longings onto others and feeling as though they have control of our lives.

By consciously choosing, we also come to see our mistakes, our weaknesses, our need for others. If we do not encounter the flaws in our own choices, we may pretend to be perfectly knowledgeable and complete in ourselves. By practicing autonomy and engaging fully with the choices we have made, we learn that we are responsible but not omniscient, that we need to admit failure and mistakes, and that we may need to change a course of action even when it is under way. We learn why and how we need others to help us in understanding ourselves and coping with the consequences of our actions. This is what I call living an intentional life.

Stories of Female Desire

In the stories of personal sovereignty in women I have told throughout this book, certain themes have recurred. The first is bringing what was hidden out into the light; the second is gaining knowledge of that which was hidden; and the third involves the paradox of autonomy—how we learn about our vulnerability and limitations when we finally become Subjects of our own desires.

In the first story Lady Ragnell lives hidden in the woods of shame, yet she knows and directs herself by her own desires, so when her moment arrives she steps out and makes her desires clear. This begins the process of her development.

In the second story Pandora digs up the buried earthenware jar and brings it into the light of day. Within it are the troubles and evils of life, including death, that divide humans from the gods. Pandora's curiosity causes her to reveal what had been hidden from men: the weaknesses that make us mortal and fallible.

In the third story Psyche shines her light on the god Amor, revealing the nature of romantic desire as an unattainable ideal and awakening the possibility for true love. Later, in pursuit of becoming a Subject of her own desires, Psyche opens the box of beauty that she brought from the underworld. Again, female curiosity leads to an uncovering: death is where beauty was supposed to be.

In the fourth story the miller's daughter reveals the savage nature of the hidden desire for power—the impotent rage of narcissism. By identifying the impish man, the daughter brings out into the light the narcissistic longings of mothers (or fathers) to amass reflected glory through their children. These longings can bring disastrous results for mother and child if both lose their capacity for autonomous development.

In the account of the Hungry Ghosts of Buddhist cosmology, we saw one more example of the importance of bringing what was hidden into the light. Our attachment to hidden longings that can never be fulfilled—such as wanting to be the youthful desire-awakening maiden when we are no longer young—binds us to pathologies of material desires, like compulsive shopping and eating.

In all these stories women gain knowledge in seeing what had been hidden. Ragnell discovers what she must master to restore her sovereignty: the rebukes to her authority and the ridicule for being a hag. Bringing her hag complex into the open, she comes to understand how to transform her wretched identity as a loathsome lady into that of a free, serene woman. In the process she also learns that she must depend on others' goodwill as well as her own authority to bring about changes.

Ultimately, Gawain grants her the "right" to exercise her autonomy in choosing how she will appear. Surrounded as she is by male dominance, Ragnell's choices and actions are intertwined with the choices and actions of her male counterparts as she struggles to claim personal sovereignty in her marriage. Because this story was probably told originally as an edifying tale about the loss of female sovereignty in traditional patriarchal marriage, we must understand it in the context of the limitations of female desire. Many women have questioned me about the fact that Gawain bestows the right to her personal sovereignty on Ragnell. I have answered that we all depend on others to assist us in finding our autonomy. In this story Ragnell depends on her partner, but she is in no way passive in her dependence. She makes every choice presented to her, and she is always clear about her authority and knowledge.

We don't know anything of Pandora's development after she opened the earthenware jar. We can only speculate that her curiosity brought her knowledge about the necessity of transformation. We might imagine that Pandora's development was similar to Psyche's. Psyche encountered two transformative moments when she gained important knowledge through uncovering what had been hidden: the first when she lifted the candle to reveal the identity of Amor, and the second when she opened the box of beauty.

In the first, knowledge brought sorrow, because at the moment that Psyche learned Amor's true identity as the god of love she lost him. Knowledge often awakens us to our limitations, sometimes even to pain and loss. Emotionally, Psyche had been wedded to a fantasy or ideal until she lifted the candle to reveal Amor; she had been in a death-marriage, in which she was passive and ignorant, even though it felt pleasurable. Without knowledge of her partner's identity, she had no freedom.

When Psyche held her candle over Amor, she illuminated her own desire to be cared for in a realm of effortless abundance. She had been trapped in a ghostly place in which her fantasies materialized into food, drink, pleasures, and sex. Faced with the recognition of how she had been living as a human in the realm of the gods, Psyche was bereft of all that she loved. Her all-too-human error of carelessly dropping hot wax on Amor's sleeping form symbolizes the impossibility of our achieving perfect pleasure and beauty. True love, as we have repeatedly seen, is possible only when desire meets reality; Psyche had no possibility of true love as long as her desire was captured by fantasy.

In her search for her lost Amor, Psyche is confronted with many tasks set by her challenger, Venus. With the help of others, Psyche overcomes obstacles and gains knowledge of herself—her instincts, her intuitions, her discriminating intellect. Each task brings greater self-awareness. But the final task, to bring Venus the box of beauty, is the only one Psyche fails. Her lingering desire to be the most beautiful of all women remained even after she had learned about many of her strengths and abilities. Psyche's death-sleep can be interpreted as a depression, an inner deadness that results from her hidden desire to remain the Object of Desire.

How can we understand her rescue by the powerful Venus? I believe that Venus represents Psyche's mother complex, a discordant source that had been driving her to be the most beautiful. Because Psyche has been struggling to defeat this powerful complex, she successfully completes all but one of the tasks. But she cannot bring about her own liberation from the spell cast by the negative complex. She has a fatal flaw (addiction to beauty) that she is unable to overcome without the aid of those more powerful than herself, Amor and Venus (who can be interpreted as separate beings or as aspects of Psyche's personality who aid her ego). However we choose to interpret the last scene of Psyche's tale, we can be certain that she is not a hero. She does not save herself, but she is saved; she has reached a frame of mind in which liberation is possible, but she cannot bring it about without help.

When the miller's daughter learns Rumpelstiltskin's name—symbolizing the knowledge that he is the discordant source of her mother's power needs—she is directly released from his spell and becomes her own person. Hearing his name spoken by the daughter, the little man tears himself into two, depicting the destruction of the daughter's Divine Child complex, which had bound her to carry out her mother's will rather than develop her own autonomy. But even here the daughter depends on the messenger to find the name of the little man; she does not find it all on her own.

The Paradox of Autonomy

BRINGING WHAT IS HIDDEN out into the light and knowing the name of what troubles us are the first steps toward autonomy. They provide us with insight and understanding about our hidden desires and emotional habits. But to become Subjects of our own desires, we need the moral strength or courage to continue to face the conflicts of our inner and outer lives as we attempt to put our insights into action. Just as Psyche's illumination of Amor and her curiosity about the box of beauty led to more struggle and challenge, so living as Subjects of our desires has the nature of conflict.

When an unmarried client of mine in her thirties recently decided to adopt an interracial baby, she did so with the recognition that many conflicts would arise from having a baby of a race different from her own. Contemplating the adoption, this woman went through a long process of asking herself and her partner questions. Many of the questions had a "What if . . ." beginning, and the client eventually saw that she was trying to protect herself and her (potential) baby from harm by trying to get guarantees before even deciding to take the baby. With my help she stopped asking these questions and instead, when she felt the impulse to ask, she breathed deeply and questioned herself, "What do I fear in this?" Discovering that her fears were human-size—Would she be a good mother? Would others criticize her for adopting a baby without being married? Would her partner leave when the baby came? Would the child turn on her because she was of a different race?—allowed my client to decide in favor of adopting. All her questions had to do with how others would perceive her rather than with the experience of loving a child. She decided she wanted the experience and could learn from the conflicts that would inevitably develop.

Another client, in her midfifties, was faced with the decision of whether to leave a marriage of thirty years when she discovered that her husband was having an affair with someone at his workplace. As she looked at what she wanted, she saw conflict: she wanted to stay and retain a sense of family and history, *and* she wanted to respect herself and move on with her own life without her husband. For several months she and I talked about the conditions that had led to her husband's desire for another woman—the lack of sex between them, the failure to engage in lively dialogue after their children grew up, the gradual separation of their lives as their personal interests diverged. My client felt responsible for a great deal of what had gone badly over the past ten years.

Her husband did not want to dissolve the marriage, but he would not promise her that he would never again engage in a sexual relationship with an outside partner. She asked him to go to couples therapy with her, and he did, but she suspected that he was continuing to be involved with his lover. Increasingly she felt that she was unable to live with so little trust in him, and she decided to leave the marriage. Although she faced a terrible grief in leaving, she was also satisfied that she had made a choice that expressed her values of honesty and trust as a foundation for a marriage. She left as the Subject of her own desires, so she did not feel ashamed and broken by her husband's infidelities, although she knew that her life ahead would be difficult in many ways.

When you live an intentional life and make your own decisions, you come to see the paradox of your personal sovereignty. To follow blindly your own desires will create a prison of constant craving and longing, from which you cannot escape. To refuse your desires will create another kind of prison, one in which you will feel ashamed, guilty, resentful, or even psychologically dead. To engage your desires, with the recognition that they will teach you about your limitations, your vulnerability, and your conflicts, as well as your strengths, will lead to the discovery of your own nature, of who you are.

I know from personal experience and my clinical work that we become deeply ethical people only through the lessons of personal sovereignty. By engaging freely in our own choices, and then seeing how and why those choices are flawed and lacking, we develop a sincere tolerance for our own and others' faults, and a generosity in wanting to help. Struggling to use our conscious intentions to guide our actions, seeing how hard it is not to be driven by our complexes and meaner desires, we develop compassion for others and ourselves. Over time these experiences teach us. Here is how Jung put it:

> The apparently unendurable conflict is proof of the rightness of your life. A life without inner contradiction is either only half a life or else is a life in the Beyond, which is destined only for angels. But God loves human beings more than the angels.

When we become Subjects of our desires, then, we do not learn how to be gods or how to get our own way. We do not become more selfish or self-interested; rather we come to see what it means to be human.

True and Authentic

PERSONAL SOVEREIGNTY LEADS to the knowledge of freedom and limitation. On the one hand, we come to consider our own desires and needs more openly, to take them as seriously as we would take those of others—our friends, children, partners. We learn to negotiate differences and conflicts among our various commitments to community, family, self, as well as differences and conflicts with others' needs and desires. On the other hand, we learn to recognize our mistakes, blindness, weaknesses, and other limitations that are not under our control. We learn that we continue to live in a male-dominated

society in which images of the desire-awakening maiden sym-
bolize an almost transcendent vitality. We learn that our own
claims to authority and desire, even when spoken calmly without blame, can be unfairly labeled as the expression of a hag-
bitch whose negative emotions are deeply threatening.

The dialogue that develops between freedom and limitation of female desire allows us to open up conversations that
we thought we could never have. These conversations inevitably show us that an authentic self depends on relationships
and contexts that we can never wholly command or control.
As the philosopher Charles Taylor plainly says, "My own identity crucially depends on my dialogical relations with others."

In my understanding of female desire, I agree wholly with
Taylor's view of the nature of authenticity: that its source
is relationship, and that some of the things we most value in
our selves are accessible to us only through those we love. So
those others become internal to our own identities. Autonomy—our ability to make choices and take responsibility for
ourselves—when understood as embedded in our relationships, leads eventually to gratitude, tolerance, and compassion
for others.

When we act according to our "true self" or "authentic
self," we make transparent our shortcomings in a way that
arouses compassion. In order to see ourselves as naked and not
to be ashamed, to acknowledge our weaknesses and know that
they open us to being loved by others, we have to engage our
own choices again and again. Following our intentions, we
come to our authentic being, and we no longer have to hide in
shame or equivocate in guilt.

As Subjects of our own desires, we develop our potentials
and grow in our capacity to lead an ethical life. What we once

accepted as the dictates of an external authority we now think out for ourselves, and we are required to articulate an identity over time that places us consistently and squarely at the center of our own contradictory feelings and motives.

Under these conditions we are not free in the sense of being more independent or more individual. But we are free in understanding human intentions and actions, our own and others', in a manner that allows us to trust our hearts. For if wanting to be wanted is about image, wanting to be loved is about heart. The heart-truth of wanting to be loved is what we discover through a way of living that rests on honesty, direct-ness, transparency. When we live as the Subjects of our desires, we discover that we are sustained by others, paradoxically through making our own choices every step of the way.

Notes

ONE. WANTING TO BE WANTED

1 **Lacan:** According to the Lacanian analyst Stuart Schneiderman, in a 1972–73 seminar titled "Encore," "Lacan was saying that, whatever it is that women want, it is not love. . . . Women do not give their love to men who love them, but to men who want them." Stuart Schneiderman, *Jacques Lacan: The Death of an Intellectual Hero* (Cambridge, Mass.: Harvard University Press, 1983), p. 30.

4 **double bind of female authority:** See Polly Young-Eisendrath and Florence Wiedemann, *Female Authority: Empowering Women Through Psychotherapy* (New York: Guilford Press, 1987).

7 **Sigmund Freud:** Rather than a hostile remark, this was a genuine inquiry into the unhappy condition of Victorian women posed by Freud to Marie Bonaparte: "The great question that has never been answered and which I have not yet been able to answer despite my thirty years of research into the feminine soul, is 'What does a woman want?'" Quoted in Lucy Freeman and Herbert S. Strean, *Freud and Women* (New York: Frederick Ungar, 1981), p. 200.

7 **medieval folktale:** See Donald Sands, "The Marriage of Sir Gawain and the Lady Ragnell," in *Middle English Verse Romances* (New York: Holt, Rinehart, and Winston, 1966).

8 **modern retelling:** See Ethel Johnston Phelps, ed., *The Maid of the North: Feminist Folk Tales from Around the World* (New York: Holt, Rinehart, and Winston, 1981); and Polly Young-Eisendrath, *Hags and Heroes: A Feminist Approach to Jungian Psychotherapy with Couples* (Toronto: Inner City Books, 1984).

14 **mythical hag:** See Young-Eisendrath, *Hags and Heroes*, pp. 65–68.

18 **anorectic woman-child:** The anorectic woman-child seems to be personified in today's models. For data on weight and height for models versus the average American woman and the average U.S. Army woman, see note to page 36, **weigh between twenty-five and thirty pounds less.**

18 **Subject:** According to Lacan, our early childhood experiences of subjectivity are chaotic and difficult to bear. Therefore, we seek to be mirrored and tend to identify with images that are more coherent than our own subjective experience. Although we all seek the coherence of a mirrored self over the chaos of a subjective self, women are especially encouraged to experience their subjectivity as objects outside themselves by locating themselves in reflections, thereby losing sight of their own true subjectivity. See Joseph H. Smith and William Kerrigan, eds., *Interpreting Lacan: Psychiatry and the Humanities*, vol. 6 (New Haven, Conn.: Yale University Press, 1983).

20 **Diana, Princess of Wales:** For a recent account of Princess Diana's last year, see Donald Spoto, *Diana: The Last Year* (New York: Harmony Books, 1997). See also Andrew Morton, *Diana: Her New Life* (New York: Simon and Schuster, 1994).

21 **"In breaking out":** Carol Gilligan, "For Many Women, Gazing at Diana Was Gazing Within," *New York Times*, September 9, 1997.

22 **Shame:** For an insightful discussion of the role of shame in human development, see Michael Lewis, *Shame: The Exposed Self* (New York: Free Press, 1995). See also Daniel L. Nathanson, ed., *The Many Faces of Shame* (New York: Guilford Press, 1987).

23 **"I just need more space":** See, for example, John Gray, *Men Are from Mars, Women Are from Venus: A Practical Guide for Improving*

Communication and Getting What You Want in Your Relationships (New York: HarperCollins, 1992).

24 **pop psychology:** Ibid. See also Robert Bly, *Iron John: A Book About Men* (Reading, Mass.: Addison-Wesley, 1990).

26 **psychological complexes:** Jung's theory of psychological complexes is presented in Carl G. Jung, "A Review of the Complex Theory," in *The Collected Works of C. G. Jung,* 2d ed., vol. 8, trans. R. F. C. Hull (Princeton, N.J.: Princeton University Press, 1969), pp. 92–104; and *Collected Works,* vol. 2, trans. L. Stein (Princeton, N.J.: Princeton University Press, 1973), pp. 598–603.

27 **emotional meanings:** See James Le Doux, *The Emotional Brain: The Mysterious Underpinnings of Emotional Life* (New York: Simon and Schuster, 1996); and Daniel Goleman, *Emotional Intelligence: Why It Can Matter More Than IQ* (New York: Bantam Books, 1995).

28 **hungry ghosts:** See note to page 138, **Hungry Ghosts.**

32 **Paracelsus:** I am quoting this material from memory. For a discussion of the relationship between knowledge and love, see Hans G. Furth, *Knowledge as Desire: An Essay on Freud and Piaget* (New York: Columbia University Press, 1987).

TWO. THE MENACE OF FEMALE BEAUTY

33 **female power is beauty:** Two excellent appraisals of the damaging effects of current images of female beauty are Naomi Wolf, *The Beauty Myth: How Images of Beauty Are Used Against Women* (New York: William Morrow, 1991); and Susan Bordo, *Unbearable Weight: Feminism, Western Culture, and the Body* (Berkeley and Los Angeles: University of California Press, 1993).

34 **problems with appearance:** See Joan Jacobs Brumberg, *The Body Project: An Intimate History of American Girls* (New York: Random House, 1997), p. 195.

35 **between the ages of thirteen and eighteen:** The self-centeredness and self-consciousness that emerge in adolescence are the natural outgrowth of a capacity for self-reflection that did not exist before. See Jean Piaget, *The Language and Thought of the Child,* trans. M. Warden (New York: Harcourt, Brace, 1926); David Elkind, "Egocentrism in Adolescence," *Child Development* 38 (1967), pp. 1025–34;

David Elkind, *Child Development and Education: A Piagetian Perspective* (New York: Oxford University Press, 1976); and David Elkind, *The Child and Society: Essays in Applied Child Development* (New York: Oxford University Press, 1979).

35 **Two-thirds of all American women:** Laura Fraser, *Losing It: America's Obsession with Weight and the Diet Industry That Feeds on It* (New York: E. P. Dutton, 1997), p. 46.

35 **$5 to $7 billion:** Ibid., p. 82.

36 **by age thirteen:** Brumberg, *Body Project*, p. xxiv. Two recent studies show that female fourth-graders are concerned about their weight. See Ann M. Gustafson-Larson and Rhonda Dale Terry, "Weight-Related Behaviors and Concerns of Fourth-Grade Children," *Journal of the American Dietetic Association* 92 (1992), pp. 818–822; and Mark H. Thelen, Anne H. Powell, Christine Lawrence, and Mark E. Kuhnert, "Eating and Body Image Concerns Among Children," *Journal of Clinical Child Psychology* 21, no. 1 (1992), pp. 60–69. See also Judith Newman, "Little Girls Who Won't Eat: The Alarming Epidemic of Eating Disorders," *Redbook*, October 1997, pp. 120–154.

36 **fasting, overuse of laxatives . . . :** See Joan P. Cesari, "Fad Bulimia: A Serious and Separate Counseling Issue," *Journal of College Student Personnel* 27, no. 3 (1986), pp. 255–259; Helen P. Klemchuk, Cheryl B. Hutchinson, and Rochelle I. Frank, "Body Dissatisfaction and Eating-Related Problems on the College Campus: Usefulness of the Eating Disorder Inventory with a Nonclinical Population," *Journal of Counseling Psychology* 37, no. 3 (1990), pp. 297–305; and Paul Rozin and April E. Fallon, "Body Images, Attitudes to Weight, and Misperceptions of Figure Preferences of the Opposite Sex: A Comparison of Men and Women in Two Generations," *Journal of Abnormal Psychology* 97, no. 3 (1988), pp. 342–345.

36 **61 percent of college women:** See Laurie B. Mintz and Nancy E. Betz, "Prevalence and Correlates of Eating Disordered Behaviors Among Undergraduate Women," *Journal of Counseling Psychology* 35, no. 4 (1988), pp. 463–471.

36 **weigh between twenty-five and thirty pounds less:** Laura Fraser reports that today's average model is "five feet nine and a half inches tall, weighs 123 pounds, wears a size 6 or 8, and often has too little body fat to menstruate. . . . The average American woman, on the

other hand, is five feet four inches, weighs 144 pounds, and wears a size 12." Fraser, *Losing It*, pp. 8–9. The Fort Military Information Command Center lists the following maximum weight standards for a five-foot, four-inch female member of the U.S. Army: ages seventeen to twenty, 133 pounds; ages twenty-one to twenty-seven, 137 pounds; ages twenty-eight to thirty-nine, 141 pounds; ages forty and above, 145 pounds. See Fort Military Information Command Center web site at http://www.fortmicc.com/pages/FMAR108.htm.

36 **viewing fifty fashion photographs:** See Bill Thornton and Jason Maurice, "Physique Contrast Effect: Adverse Impact of Idealized Body Images for Women," *Sex Roles* 37, nos. 6–7 (September 1997), pp. 433–439. See also Sarah Grogan, Zoe Williams, and Mark Conner, "The Effects of Viewing Same-Gender Photographic Models on Body-Esteem," *Psychology of Women Quarterly* 20, no. 4 (1996), pp. 569–575.

37 **thirty minutes of watching TV:** See Philip N. Myers, Jr., "The Elastic Body Image: The Effect of Television Advertising and Programming on Body Image Distortions in Young Women," *Journal of Communication* 42, no. 3 (Summer 1992), pp. 108–133.

37 **women over sixty:** See Sara Wilcox, "Age and Gender in Relation to Body Attitudes: Is There a Double Standard of Aging?" *Psychology of Women Quarterly* 21, no. 4 (1997), pp. 549–565.

38 **"Being thin":** Fraser, *Losing It*, p. 7.

39 **history of female thinness:** ibid., pp. 16–49. See also Brumberg, *Body Project*.

40 **supermodels:** For a comprehensive exposé of the lives of celebrity models, see Michael Gross, *Model: The Ugly Business of Beautiful Women* (New York: Warner Books, 1996).

40 **survey of third-graders:** I heard about this survey at a conference on eating disorders, where it was reported as part of a presentation by members of an eating disorders clinic in Cambridge, Massachusetts.

40 **"third job":** See Fraser, *Losing It*, p. 7.

41 **girdles and corsets:** For a history of the transition from external to internal corsets, see ibid., pp. 16–49; and Brumberg, *Body Project*.

41 **Studies have proven:** Laura Fraser reports studies performed by Steven Blair of the Cooper Institute for Aerobics Research in Dallas,

Texas, which indicate that "as long as they're in good shape, someone who's overweight by 20, 30 or even 75 pounds is at no particular health risk." Fraser, *Losing It*, p. 250. For information on U.S. Army female weight standards, see note to page 36, **weigh between twenty-five and thirty pounds less.**

42 **"Man aspires . . .":** Simone de Beauvoir, *The Second Sex* (New York: Vintage Books, 1989), trans. H. M. Parshley, pp. 80–81.

43 **certain sociobiologists:** See, for example, Richard Dawkins, *The Selfish Gene* (New York: Oxford University Press, 1989); and Edward O. Wilson, *Sociobiology: The New Synthesis* (Cambridge, Mass.: Harvard University Press, 1975).

44 **Hesiod:** See Hesiod, *The Works and the Days; Theogony; The Shield of Herakles*, trans. Richmond Lattimore (Ann Arbor: University of Michigan Press, 1959).

47 **"willing victim":** See Spoto, *Diana, The Last Year*, p. 57.

47 **freedom of appearance:** Sadly enough, among the consequences of middle-class adolescent girls' deliberately dressing for their own comfort as opposed to dressing for boys' pleasure is rejection from boys, as well as the severing of relationships with their female peers who conform to current fashion trends. See Lyn Mikel Brown, *Raising Their Voices: The Politics of Girls' Anger* (Cambridge, Mass.: Harvard University Press, 1998).

48 **dividing women among themselves:** Elizabeth Debold, Marie C. Wilson, and Idelisse Malave argue that the roots of the often cruel competitiveness among women lie in a detrimental mother-daughter separation in early adolescence, prescribed by models of child development largely created by and for males. As girls give up their connectedness with their mothers, they give up the potential for intimate knowledge of their own desires and consequently turn to relationships endorsed by patriarchal culture. Giving up what they know—that is, the injustice of a world that favors men over women—girls try desperately "to keep from being abandoned or excluded by their mothers and the other women closest to them" and thus "try to live up to the impossible ideal of the Perfect Girl. They act out their anger covertly through increasingly painful games of inclusion and exclusion." Debold, Wilson, and Malave, *The Mother-Daughter Revolution: From Betrayal to Power* (Reading,

Mass.: Addison-Wesley, 1993), p. 43. Drawing on the Brazilian educator and social activist Paulo Freire's concept of "horizontal violence," Lyn Mikel Brown observes that the lack of mutual support and solidarity among women is a consequence of the internalization of the values of the divisive, dominant patriarchal culture. See Brown, *Raising Their Voices*.

49 **Feminist commentators:** In the spate of commentaries on popular media during the latter part of 1998, I heard a number of feminist journalists and academics speak to the issue of Monica Lewinsky being the "other woman." In general, feminist sympathies were not with Lewinsky.

THREE. SEX THROUGH THE LOOKING GLASS

58 **"crossing the boundaries . . .":** Otto Kernberg, *Love Relations: Normality and Pathology* (New Haven, Conn.: Yale University Press, 1995), p. 43.

58 **Most national surveys:** See Shere Hite, *The Hite Report* (New York: Macmillan, 1976); Dianne Grosskopf, *Sex and the Married Woman* (New York: Simon and Schuster, 1983); and "Who, What, Where, and How Do You Love?" *Redbook*, October 1989, p. 134. For more recent, comprehensive data on sexual behavior in American society, see June M. Reinisch, *The Kinsey Institute New Report on Sex: What You Must Know to Be Sexually Literate* (New York: St. Martin's Press, 1990); and Robert T. Michael, John H. Gagnon, Edward O. Laumann, and Gina Kolata, *Sex in America: A Definitive Survey* (Boston and New York: Little, Brown, 1994).

59 **lesbian relationships:** See David Farley Hurlbert and Carol Apt, "Female Sexuality: A Comparative Study Between Women in Homosexual and Heterosexual Relationships," *Journal of Sex and Marital Therapy* 19, no. 4 (1993), pp. 315–327.

59 ***You're Not What I Expected:*** See Polly Young-Eisendrath, *You're Not What I Expected: Learning to Love the Opposite Sex* (New York: William Morrow, 1993).

60 **lack of female sexual pleasure:** See surveys quoted above in note to page 58, **Most national surveys.** See also David Farley Hurlbert, Carol Apt, and Sarah Meyers Rabehl, "Key Variables to Understanding Female Sexual Satisfaction: An Examination of Women in

Nondistressed Marriages," *Journal of Sex and Marital Therapy* 19, no. 2 (1993), pp. 154–165; Raymond C. Rosen, Jennifer B. Taylor, Sandra R. Leiblum, and Gloria A. Bachmann, "Prevalence of Sexual Dysfunction in Women: Results of a Survey Study of 329 Women in an Outpatient Gynecological Clinic," *Journal of Sex and Marital Therapy* 19, no. 3 (1993), pp. 171–188; and David Farley Hurlbert and Carol Apt, "Female Sexual Desire, Response, and Behavior," *Behavior Modification* 18, no. 4 (1994), pp. 488–504.

61 **Naomi Wolf:** *Promiscuities: The Secret Struggle for Womanhood* (New York: Random House, 1997).

61 **Renaldus Columbus:** Ibid., p. 143.

62 **"maternal instinct":** Ibid., p. 146.

62 **"for different reasons . . .":** Hurlbert and Apt, "Female Sexual Desire," p. 494.

63 **physically abusive relationships:** Ibid., p. 495.

63 **"The relationship . . .":** Ibid., p. 496.

67 **sexual fantasies that are disturbing:** Wendy Maltz and Suzie Boss, *In the Garden of Desire: The Intimate World of Women's Sexual Fantasies* (New York: Broadway Books, 1997), pp. 194–195.

68 **contemporary translation:** See Michael Grant, *Myths of the Greeks and the Romans* (New York: New American Library, Mentor, 1962), pp. 357–362.

68 **Carol Gilligan:** See Carol Gilligan, "The Riddle of Femininity and the Psychology of Love," in Willard Gaylin and Ethel Person, eds., *Passionate Attachments: Thinking About Love* (New York: Free Press, 1988), pp. 101–114.

68 **Florence Wiedemann and myself:** See Polly Young-Eisendrath and Florence Wiedemann, *Female Authority: Empowering Women Through Psychotherapy* (New York: Guilford Press, 1987).

75 **Psyche's own complex:** For a Jungian interpretation of the myth, see ibid.

81 **Octavio Paz:** As discussed in Kernberg, *Love Relations*, p. 44.

81 **deeply known to each other:** See note to page 32, **Paracelsus.**

FOUR. HOTHOUSE MOTHERING AND THE DIVINE CHILD

84 **Idealizing motherhood:** For a recent discussion of the excessive blame placed on today's mothers, see Diane Eyer, *Motherguilt: How Our Culture Blames Mothers for What's Wrong with Society* (New York: Times Books, 1996). For a critical analysis of the post–World War II glorification of full-time motherhood and housework, see Betty Friedan's seminal work, *The Feminine Mystique* (New York: W. W. Norton, 1963).

85 **singular importance of Mother:** Writing about male clients, the Jungian analyst Guy Corneau argues that the very absence of fathers in family life reveals how relevant their role is: "Although the literature of psychoanalysis has abundantly described the influence of mothers on their sons, it has in this regard often neglected to mention that these mothers were omnipresent and omnipotent precisely because the fathers were absent—so absent, in fact, that their absence was simply taken for granted. These days, when I hear my patients complain about their mothers, what I also hear (although it is not stated explicitly) is that their fathers were absent." Guy Corneau, *Absent Fathers, Lost Sons: The Search for Masculine Identity*, trans. Larry Shouldice (Boston: Shambhala, 1991), p. 16. Elizabeth Debold, Marie C. Wilson, and Idelisse Malave contend that mother blaming has emerged in our society over the past hundred years as a middle- and upper-class phenomenon: "Very little effort is made in traditional therapies to explore the complexities of a mother's behavior, place it in the appropriate socioeconomic or political context, or wonder about her partner's role (or lack of it)." Debold, Wilson, and Malave, *The Mother-Daughter Revolution: From Betrayal to Power* (Reading, Mass.: Addison-Wesley, 1993), p. 22. A recent book, based on extensive empirical and statistical analyses, claims that peers are more important than parents in the long-term development of the child's personality; see Judith Rich Harris, *The Nurture Assumption: Why Children Turn Out the Way They Do* (New York: Free Press, 1998).

86 **collective inability:** With the loss of extended family and communal life, it is little wonder that motherhood "is exhausting in our society. . . . Motherhood does not have to be the responsibility solely of biological or adoptive mothers living in the isolation of individual nuclear families." Debold, Wilson, and Malave, *Mother-*

Daughter Revolution, p. 235. For a discussion of less individualized and more socialized forms of child care, such as what exists in Sweden, see Eyer, *Motherguilt*.

88 **"That calm, sure . . .":** Adrienne Rich, *Of Woman Born: Motherhood as Experience and Institution* (New York: W. W. Norton, 1976), pp. 35–36.

91 **mothering as distinct from motherhood:** See ibid.

91 **Ann Dally:** See Ann Dally, *Inventing Motherhood: The Consequences of an Ideal* (New York: Schocken Books, 1982).

92 **"When large numbers . . .":** Ibid., p. 10.

92 **"the era of unbroken . . .":** Ibid.

93 **hothouse isolation:** For a critique of the compartmentalization of mothers and motherhood in isolated nuclear family units and a suggested alternative of shared, supportive mothering through circles of "othermothers," see Debold, Wilson, and Malave, *Mother-Daughter Revolution*, pp. 223–246.

96 **only recently invented:** For a history of the emergence of childhood as a social phenomenon, see also Philippe Ariès, *Centuries of Childhood: A Social History of Family Life*, trans. Robert Baldick (New York: Alfred A. Knopf, 1962). A brief outline of Ariès's main ideas may be found in Shulamith Firestone, *The Dialectic of Sex* (New York: William Morrow, 1970), pp. 81–118.

97 **"true motherhood":** Dally, *Inventing Motherhood*, p. 17.

100 **expert advice:** for a critique of the effect of "expert advice" on child rearing as it pertains to female children, see Carol Gilligan, *In a Different Voice: Psychological Theory and Women's Development* (Cambridge, Mass.: Harvard University Press, 1982). See also Barbara Ehrenreich and Deirdre English, *For Her Own Good: 150 Years of the Experts' Advice to Women* (New York: Doubleday, Anchor Press, 1978).

100 **two-thirds of all American mothers:** Arlie P. Hochschild, *The Second Shift: Working Parents and the Revolution at Home* (New York: Viking Press, 1989), p. 2.

100 **thirty-five hours or more weekly:** Ibid.

101 **"second shift":** See note to page 124, **ideals of perfection.**

101 **attachment theory:** For a recent critical overview of classical attachment theory, see Tiffany Field, "Attachment and Separation in Young Children," *Annual Review of Psychology* 47 (1996), pp. 541–561.

101 **Rene Spitz and John Bowlby:** See Rene A. Spitz, *The First Year of Life: A Psychoanalytic Study of Normal and Deviant Development of Object Relations* (New York: International Universities Press, 1965); and John Bowlby, *Child Care and the Growth of Love*, 2d ed. (Baltimore: Penguin Books, 1965); Bowlby, *Attachment and Loss*, vol. 1 (London: Hogarth Press, 1969); Bowlby, *A Secure Base: Parent-Child Attachment and Healthy Human Development* (New York: Basic Books, 1988).

102 **Mary Main:** See Mary Main, "Exploration, Play, and Cognitive Functioning Related to Infant-Mother Attachment," *Infant Behavior and Development* 6, no. 2 (1983), pp. 167–174; "Recent Studies in Attachment: Overview, with Selected Implications for Clinical Work," in *Attachment Theory: Social, Developmental, and Clinical Perspectives*, ed. Susan Goldberg, Roy Muir, and John Kerr (Hillsdale, N.J.: Analytic Press, 1995); "Discourse, Prediction, and Recent Studies in Attachment: Implications for Psychoanalysis," in *Research in Psychoanalysis: Process, Development, Outcome*, ed. Theodore Shapiro and Robert N. Emde (Madison, Conn.: International Universities Press, 1995). See also Mary D. S. Ainsworth, M. C. Blehar, E. Waters, and S. Wall, *Patterns of Attachment: A Psychological Study of the Strange Situation* (Hillsdale, N.J.: Lawrence Erlbaum, 1978).

102 **misleading to use these findings:** A recent National Institute of Child Health and Human Development (NICHD) study suggests that, in and of itself, nonmaternal child care is neither beneficial nor detrimental to infant-mother attachments with respect to specific infant-mother separations. See NICHD Early Child Care Research Network, "The Effects of Infant Child Care on Infant-Mother Attachment Security: Results of the NICHD Study of Early Child Care," *Child Development* 68, no. 5 (1997), pp. 860–879.

103 **"Two centuries ago . . .":** Dally, *Inventing Motherhood*, pp. 26–27.

103 **"One cannot grieve . . .":** Ibid., pp. 101–102.

104 **"He feels that . . .":** Ibid., p. 28.

105 **Joan Peters:** See Joan Peters, *When Mothers Work: Loving Our Children Without Sacrificing Our Selves* (Reading, Mass.: Addison-Wesley, 1997).

106 **"Divine Child":** Examples of this archetype are the Christ Child and the child who is chosen as successor to the Dalai Lama by recognizing the identifying signs. A firstborn or long-awaited child may also evoke a Divine Child archetype when the parents feel they have given birth to an extraordinary individual. For a psychological analysis of this archetype, see Erich Neumann, *The Child* (Boston: Shambhala, 1990); and Carl G. Jung, *Collected Works*, 2d ed., vol. 9, pt. 1, trans. R. F. C. Hull (Princeton, N.J.: Princeton University Press, 1969).

106 *Archetype:* See Carl G. Jung. For a thorough analysis of the evolution of Jung's concept of the archetype, see Polly Young-Eisendrath and James A. Hall, *Jung's Self Psychology: A Constructivist Perspective* (New York: Guilford Press, 1991).

106 **psychological complex:** See note to page 26, **psychological complexes.**

108 **so powerless and subordinate:** Shulamith Firestone argues that, for all practical purposes, children make up a lower class. For a discussion of children's prolonged economic and physical dependence as well as their sexual, familial, and educational repression, see Firestone, *Dialectic of Sex*, pp. 107–118.

112 **"discordant source":** Neville Symington, *Narcissism: A New Theory* (London: Karnac Books, 1997), pp. 118–119.

113 **Brothers Grimm:** See *The Complete Grimm's Fairy Tales* (New York: Random House, 1972), pp. 264–268.

117 **Elizabeth Debold, Marie Wilson, and Idelisse Malave:** See Debold, Wilson, and Malave, *Mother-Daughter Revolution*.

117 **"Ironically and tragically . . .":** Ibid., p. 55.

117 **"compromise girls' self-love . . .":** Ibid., p. 60.

119 **the word *just*:** See Symington, *Narcissism*, p. 116.

119 **"While the demands . . .":** Debold, Wilson, and Malave, *Mother-Daughter Revolution*, p. 115.

FIVE. THE MATERIAL GIRL AND THE HUNGRY GHOST

123 **Grace Baruch and Rosalind Barnett:** See Grace K. Baruch, Rosalind C. Barnett, and Caryl Rivers, *Life Prints: New Patterns of Life and Work for Today's Woman* (New York: McGraw-Hill, 1983).

124 **women's satisfaction in life:** Ibid. One recent study indicates that professional-managerial mothers report higher levels of psychological well-being than working-class and unemployed mothers. See Mary Secret and Robert G. Green, "Occupational Status Differences Among Three Groups of Married Mothers," *Affilia* 13, no. 1 (1998), pp. 47–68. Statistical trends over the last two to three decades regarding mothers in the workplace suggest that job satisfaction is the best predictor of psychological well-being. See Phyllis Moen, *Women's Two Roles: A Contemporary Dilemma* (Westport, Conn.: Auburn House, 1992).

124 **ideals of perfection:** Believing it is their personal problem rather than society's, many American women who work outside the home feel guilty and inadequate when they are unable to fulfill unrealistic child-care and housekeeping standards. This feeling is partly caused by the media, which convey the message that supermoms are personally "organized enough" to manage a perfect balancing act of home and work in a society that does not favor such integration. See Arlie P. Hochschild, *The Second Shift: Working Parents and the Revolution at Home* (New York: Viking Press, 1989). In a study of dual-career couples in the corporate world, sociologist Rosanna Hertz calls corporate employers the "silent partners" in dual-career marriages, who do nothing to facilitate but, on the contrary, often sabotage the marriage. See Hertz, *More Equal Than Others: Women and Men in Dual-Career Marriages* (Berkeley and Los Angeles: University of California Press, 1986).

125 **seventy-six cents:** Ginia Bellafante, "Feminism: It's All About Me!" *Time*, June 29, 1998, p. 58.

126 **"One woman, divorcing . . .":** Marcia Millman, *Warm Hearts and Cold Cash: The Intimate Dynamics of Families and Money* (New York: Free Press, 1991), p. 135.

128 **"Everything she does . . .":** Deborah Tannen, *Talking from Nine to Five: Women and Men in the Workplace: Language, Sex, and Power* (New York: William Morrow, 1994), p. 203.

129 **conversational rituals:** See ibid.

130 **more indirect:** Deborah Tannen argues that both women and men engage in indirect communication: "Most studies finding women to be more indirect are about getting others to do things. . . . But the situations in which men are most often found to be indirect have to do with the expression of weakness, problems, and errors, and of emotions other than anger." Ibid., pp. 89–90.

130 **"there is an expectation . . .":** Ibid., p. 169.

132 **Mature dependence:** W. Ronald Fairbairn, *Psychoanalytic Studies of the Personality* (Boston: Routledge and Kegan Paul, 1952), p. 41.

133 **Couples who pool:** See Philip Blumstein and Pepper Schwartz, *American Couples* (New York: William Morrow, 1983).

133 **Lesbian couples:** Ibid.

136 **shopping and consumer spending:** For a fascinating history of women's shopping patterns in the nineteenth century, see Elaine S. Abelson, *When Ladies Go A-Thieving: Middle-Class Shoplifters in the Victorian Department Store* (New York: Oxford University Press, 1989).

136 **department stores:** Ibid.

137 **especially clothes:** When so many women perceive their bodies as far less than the ideal, media-promoted norm, it is not surprising that female compulsive shoppers usually buy items related to body image, such as clothes, jewelry, and cosmetics, in an attempt to assuage depression, feelings of emptiness, and low self-esteem. See Helga Dittmar, Jane Beattie, and Susanne Friesse, "Objects, Decision Considerations, and Self-Image in Men's and Women's Impulse Purchases," *Acta Psychologica* 93, nos. 1–3 (1996), pp. 187–206; Gary A. Christenson et al., "Compulsive Buying: Descriptive Characteristics and Psychiatric Comorbidity," *Journal of Clinical Psychiatry* 55, no. 1 (January 1994), pp. 5–11; and Michel Lejoyeux, Jean Adès, Valérie Tassain, and Jacquelyn Solomon, "Phenomenology and Psychopathology of Uncontrolled Buying," *American Journal of Psychiatry* 153, no. 12 (December 1996), pp. 1524–29.

137 **it appears to offer choices:** Ibid. See also Abelson, *When Ladies Go A-Thieving*.

138 **Wheel of Life:** See L. Austine Waddell, *Tibetan Buddhism: With Its Mystic Cults, Symbolism, and Mythology* (New York: Dover, 1972).

For a discussion of the Wheel of Life from a psychological point of view, see Mark Epstein, *Thoughts Without a Thinker: Psychotherapy from a Buddhist Perspective* (New York: Basic Books, 1995).

138 **Hungry Ghosts:** For a discussion of the realm of Hungry Ghosts from a psychological point of view, see Epstein, *Thoughts Without a Thinker*, pp. 28–31.

142 **roughly $10 billion per year:** Jeanie Russell, "Klepto Nation," *Allure*, February 1998, p. 129.

142 **"I can go . . .":** Ibid., p. 131.

142 **Will Cupchik:** See William Cupchik, *Why Honest People Shoplift or Commit Other Acts of Theft: Assessment of Atypical Offenders* (Toronto: Tagami Communications, 1997).

143 **"have uncovered a terrible emptiness . . .":** Epstein, *Thoughts Without a Thinker*, p. 28.

143 **"Jackie's expenditure of . . .":** Donald W. Black, "Compulsive Buying: A Review," *Journal of Clinical Psychiatry* 57, supp. 8 (1996), p. 50.

143 **8.1 percent of the American population:** Reported ibid., p. 51.

144 **Compulsive buying is distinguished:** Ibid.

144 **about 22 percent of their income:** Reported ibid., p. 53.

145 **"It is well established . . .":** Dittmar, Beattie, and Friesse, "Objects, Decision Considerations, and Self-Image," p. 204.

147 **"longing for inexhaustible abundance . . .":** Epstein, *Thoughts Without a Thinker*, p. 30.

SIX. THE SPIRITUAL PROBLEM OF GIVING YOUR SELF AWAY

155 **TV and movies:** No doubt the heavy reliance on television and movies for general information has contributed to a loss of what the ecofeminist Charlene Spretnak has referred to as "religious literacy": "the widely acknowledged 'dumbing down' trend in American textbooks and education during the past twenty years seems to have spread to religious literacy as well." Charlene Spretnak, *States of Grace: The Recovery of Meaning in the Postmodern Age* (San Francisco: HarperCollins, 1991), p. 3.

157 **Carl Jung:** See Carl G. Jung, *Psychology and Religion* (New Haven, Conn.: Yale University Press, 1938).

157 **Robert Jay Lifton:** See Robert Jay Lifton, *The Broken Connection: On Death and the Continuity of Life* (New York: Basic Books, 1979).

163 **"The Western psychological notion . . .":** Mark Epstein, *Going to Pieces Without Falling Apart: A Buddhist Perspective on Wholeness* (New York: Broadway Books, 1998), pp. xv–xvi.

165 **"tends to be more accepting . . .":** Demaris S. Wehr, "When Good People Do Bad Things: Spiritual Abuse," in Polly Young-Eisendrath and Mel Miller, eds., *Integrity, Wisdom, and Transcendence* (London: Routledge, 2000).

165 **"to move God . . .":** Ibid.

167 **"Wild Geese":** Mary Oliver, *New and Selected Poems* (Boston: Beacon Press, 1992), p. 110.

168 **"Even my pain . . .":** Joanna Macy, *World as Lover, World as Self* (Berkeley: Parallax Press, 1991), p. 63.

168 **Starhawk:** See Starhawk, *Dreaming the Dark: Magic, Sex, and Politics* (Boston: Beacon Press, 1982), and *The Spiral Dance: A Rebirth of the Ancient Religion of the Great Goddess* (New York: Harper and Row, 1979).

169 **feminist spirituality:** Feminist spirituality is not exclusive to any one tradition. For an excellent source of feminist spirituality from different perspectives, see Judith Plaskow and Carol P. Christ, eds., *Weaving the Visions: New Patterns in Feminist Spirituality* (San Francisco: HarperSanFrancisco, 1989). See also Carol P. Christ, *Rebirth of the Goddess: Finding Meaning in Feminist Spirituality* (Reading, Mass.: Addison-Wesley, 1997); Christ, *Return of the Great Goddess* (Boston: Shambhala, 1994); and Spretnak, *States of Grace*.

171 **"Because patriarchal religions . . .":** Rita M. Gross, *Buddhism After Patriarchy* (New York: State University of New York Press, 1993), p. 282.

174 **Carol Christ and Judith Plaskow:** Carol P. Christ and Judith Plaskow, eds., *Womanspirit Rising: A Feminist Reader in Religion* (San Francisco: Harper and Row, 1979).

174 **"If God is male":** Mary Daly, *Beyond God the Father: Toward a Philosophy of Women's Liberation* (Boston: Beacon Press, 1973), p. 19.

175 **"present a growing threat":** Christ and Plaskow, *Womanspirit Rising*, p. 57.

176 **"The institutional changes . . .":** Rachel Josefowitz Siegel, "'I Don't Know Enough': Jewish Women's Learned Ignorance," in *Celebrating the Lives of Jewish Women*, ed. Siegel and Ellen Cole (New York: Haworth Press, 1997), p. 208. Web site version at http://www.utoronto.ca/wjudaism/journal/v1n1sieg.htm.

176 *bat mitzvah:* For a simple, brief description of the *bat mitzvah*, see Barbara Diamond Goldin, "Coming of Age in Judaism," *New Moon: The Magazine for Girls and Their Dreams* 5, no. 5 (1998), pp. 20–21.

177 **"As I learned more . . .":** Siegel, "I Don't Know Enough," p. 207.

178 **"To ordain women . . .":** Mary E. Hunt, "Psychological Implications of Women's Spiritual Health," *Women and Therapy* 16, nos. 2–3 (1995), p. 27.

178 **"The major change . . .":** Ibid.

178 **Nancy Mairs:** See Nancy Mairs, *Ordinary Time: Cycles in Marriage, Faith, and Renewal* (Boston: Beacon Press, 1993).

179 **Women were priests:** See Karen Jo Torjesen, *When Women Were Priests: Women's Leadership in the Early Church and the Scandal of Their Subordination in the Rise of Christianity* (San Francisco: HarperSanFrancisco, 1993).

179 **United Church of Christ:** The first fully ordained woman in the United Church of Christ was Antoinette Brown in 1853. In the United States there are currently 2,346 fully ordained women and 7,962 fully ordained men in the United Church of Christ. Information provided via telephone communication by the Research Department, United Church of Christ Board for Homeland Ministry, (216) 736-3813. Mailing address: 770 Prospect Avenue, Cleveland, Ohio 44115.

179 **Episcopal Church:** See Louie Crew, "Female Priests in the Episcopal Church," at http://newark.rutgers.edu/%7elcrew/womenpr.html.

180 **"ambivalent about acting . . .":** Siegel, "I Don't Know Enough," p. 208.

180 **first woman rabbi:** See Joseph Telushkin, "Women Rabbis," in Telushkin, *Jewish Literacy: The Most Important Things to Know About*

the Jewish Religion, Its People, and History (New York: William Morrow, 1991), pp. 428–429.

180 **Feminist Jewish study and Rosh Chodesh groups:** See Siegel, "I Don't Know Enough."

181 **"songs of triumph":** Gross, *Buddhism After Patriarchy.*

181 **"believed that women . . .":** Ibid., p. 18.

181 **daily physical work:** In Zen Buddhism guidelines for physical work have usually emerged from male monastic environments. Never considered inferior to intellectual or artistic pursuits, physical work is highly valued in Zen Buddhism and is regarded as a powerful aid to spiritual training. In thirteenth-century Japan, Zen Master Dogen wrote a manual, *Instructions for the Head Cook,* which draws parallels between meal preparation and spiritual training. See Dogen, "Instruction for the Tenzo," trans. Arnold Kotler and Kazuaki Tanahashi, in *Moon in a Dewdrop: Writings of Zen Master Dogen,* ed. Kazuaki Tanahashi (San Francisco: North Point Press, 1985), pp. 53–66. For an account of daily Zen monastic life, see Daisetz Teitaro Suzuki, *The Training of the Zen Buddhist Monk* (New York: University Books, 1959).

182 **Contemporary feminist Buddhists:** For feminist applications of Buddhist principles in everyday life, see, for example, Anne Carolyn Klein, *Meeting the Great Bliss Queen: Buddhists, Feminists, and the Art of Self* (Boston: Beacon Press, 1995); Joanna Macy, *World as Lover, World as Self* (Berkeley: Parallax Press, 1991); and Charlotte Joko Beck, *Everyday Zen: Love and Work,* ed. Steve Smith (San Francisco: HarperSanFrancisco, 1989).

182 **Margot Adler:** See Margot Adler, *Drawing Down the Moon: Witches, Pagans, Druids, Goddess-Worshipers, and Other Pagans in America Today* (Boston: Beacon Press, 1979).

183 **Goddess-based spirituality:** Although Neo-Paganism includes various forms of Goddess-based spirituality, such spirituality is not unique to Neo-Paganism. A recent anthology that provides a good overview of contemporary women's spirituality is Charlene Spretnak, ed., *The Politics of Women's Spirituality: Essays by Founding Mothers of the Movement* (New York: Anchor Books, 1994). Scholarly studies of Goddess worship and egalitarian societies in

Neolithic Europe are Marija Gimbutas, *The Goddesses and Gods of Old Europe: 6500–3500 B.C.: Myths and Cult Images* (Berkeley and Los Angeles: University of California Press, 1982); Gimbutas, *The Language of the Goddess: Unearthing the Hidden Symbols of Western Civilization* (San Francisco: Harper and Row, 1989); Gimbutas, *The Civilization of the Goddess: The World of Old Europe* (San Francisco: HarperSanFrancisco, 1991); and Riane Eisler, *The Chalice and the Blade: Our History, Our Future* (San Francisco: HarperSanFrancisco, 1987). For a history of the Goddess from the ancient Near East to Christian Europe, see Tikva Frymer-Kensky, *In the Wake of the Goddesses: Women, Culture, and the Biblical Transformation of Pagan Myth* (New York: Free Press, 1992).

185 **"We are not pitiful creatures . . .":** Mairs, *Ordinary Time*, p. 186.

SEVEN. THE PARADOX OF FREEDOM AND DESIRE

190 **"My actions . . .":** As quoted by Joan Halifax, "The Great Matter of Life and Death," *Tricycle: The Buddhist Review* 7, no. 1 (1997), p. 20.

204 **"The apparently unendurable conflict . . .":** Carl G. Jung, *Letters: 1906–1950*, vol. 1, trans. R. F. C. Hull and ed. G. Adler (Princeton, N.J.: Princeton University Press, 1973), p. 375.

205 **"My own identity . . .":** Charles Taylor, *The Ethics of Authenticity* (Cambridge, Mass.: Harvard University Press, 1991), p. 48.

Bibliography

Abelson, Elaine S. *When Ladies Go A-Thieving: Middle-Class Shoplifters in the Victorian Department Store.* New York: Oxford University Press, 1989.

Adler, Margot. *Drawing Down the Moon: Witches, Pagans, Druids, Goddess-Worshipers, and Other Pagans in America Today.* Boston: Beacon Press, 1979.

Ainsworth, Mary D. S., M. C. Blehar, E. Waters, and S. Wall. *Patterns of Attachment: A Psychological Study of the Strange Situation.* Hillsdale, N.J.: Lawrence Erlbaum, 1978.

American Association of University Women. *Shortchanging Girls, Shortchanging America.* Washington, D.C.: Greenberg-Lake, 1991.

Ariès, Philippe. *Centuries of Childhood: A Social History of Family Life.* Trans. Robert Baldick. New York: Alfred A. Knopf, 1962.

Baruch, Grace K., and Rosalind C. Barnett. "Role Quality, Multiple Role Involvement, and Psychological Well-Being in Midlife Women." *Journal of Personality and Social Psychology* 51 (1986), pp. 578–585.

Baruch, Grace K., Rosalind C. Barnett, and Caryl Rivers. *Life Prints: New Patterns of Life and Work for Today's Woman*. New York: McGraw-Hill, 1983.

Beauvoir, Simone de. *The Second Sex*. Trans. H. M. Parshley. New York: Vintage Books, 1989.

Beck, Charlotte Joko. *Everyday Zen: Love and Work*. Ed. Steve Smith. San Francisco: HarperSanFrancisco, 1989.

Bellafante, Ginia. "Feminism: It's All About Me!" *Time*, June 29, 1998.

Benvenuto, Bice. *The Works of Jacques Lacan: An Introduction*. New York: St. Martin's Press, 1986.

Black, Donald W. "Compulsive Buying: A Review." *Journal of Clinical Psychiatry* 57, supp. 8 (1996), pp. 50–54.

Blumstein, Philip, and Pepper Schwartz. *American Couples*. New York: William Morrow, 1983.

Bly, Robert. *Iron John: A Book About Men*. Reading, Mass.: Addison-Wesley, 1990.

Bordo, Susan. *Unbearable Weight: Feminism, Western Culture, and the Body*. Berkeley and Los Angeles: University of California Press, 1993.

Bowlby, John. *Attachment and Loss*. Vol 1. London: Hogarth Press, 1969.

———. *Child Care and the Growth of Love*. 2d ed. Baltimore: Penguin Books, 1965.

———. *A Secure Base: Parent-Child Attachment and Healthy Human Development*. New York: Basic Books, 1988.

Brown, Lyn Mikel. *Raising Their Voices: The Politics of Girls' Anger*. Cambridge, Mass.: Harvard University Press, 1998.

Brown, Lyn Mikel, and Carol Gilligan. *Meeting at the Crossroads: Women's Psychology and Girls' Development*. Cambridge, Mass.: Harvard University Press, 1992.

Brumberg, Joan Jacobs. *The Body Project: An Intimate History of American Girls*. New York: Random House, 1997.

Cesari, Joan P. "Fad Bulimia: A Serious and Separate Counseling Issue." *Journal of College Student Personnel* 27, no. 3 (1986), pp. 255–259.

Christ, Carol P. *Rebirth of the Goddess: Finding Meaning in Feminist Spirituality*. Reading, Mass.: Addison-Wesley, 1997.

————. *Return of the Great Goddess*. Boston: Shambhala, 1994.

Christ, Carol, and Judith Plaskow, eds. *Womanspirit Rising: A Feminist Reader in Religion*. San Francisco: Harper and Row, 1979.

Christenson, Gary A., et al. "Compulsive Buying: Descriptive Characteristics and Psychiatric Comorbidity." *Journal of Clinical Psychiatry* 55, no. 1 (January 1994), pp. 5–11.

The Complete Grimm's Fairy Tales. New York: Random House, 1972.

Corneau, Guy. *Absent Fathers, Lost Sons: The Search for Masculine Identity*. Trans. Larry Shouldice. Boston: Shambhala, 1991.

Crew, Louie. "Female Priests in the Episcopal Church." Web site at http://newark.rutgers.edu/%7elcrew/womenpr.html.

Cupchik, William. *Why Honest People Shoplift or Commit Other Acts of Theft: Assessment of Atypical Offenders*. Toronto: Tagami Communications, 1997.

Dally, Ann. *Inventing Motherhood: The Consequences of an Ideal*. New York: Schocken Books, 1982.

Daly, Mary. *Beyond God the Father: Toward a Philosophy of Women's Liberation*. Boston: Beacon Press, 1973.

Daniels-Beirness, T. "Measuring Peer Status in Boys and Girls: A Problem of Apples and Oranges." In B. H. Schneider, G. Attili, J. Nadel, and R. P. Weissberg, eds. *Social Competence in Developmental Perspective*. 2d ed. Boston: Kluwer, 1989.

Dawkins, Richard. *The Selfish Gene*. New York: Oxford University Press, 1989.

Debold, Elizabeth, Marie C. Wilson, and Idelisse Malave. *The Mother-Daughter Revolution: From Betrayal to Power*. Reading, Mass.: Addison-Wesley, 1993.

Dittmar, Helga, Jane Beattie, and Susanne Friesse. "Objects, Decision Considerations, and Self-Image in Men's and Women's Impulse Purchases." *Acta Psychologica* 93, nos. 1–3 (1996), pp. 187–206.

Dogen. "Instruction for the Tenzo." Trans. Arnold Kotler and Kazuaki Tanahashi. In *Moon in a Dewdrop: Writings of Zen Master Dogen*, ed. Kazuaki Tanahashi. San Francisco: North Point Press, 1985, pp. 53–66.

Ehrenreich, Barbara. "The Week Feminists Got Laryngitis." *Time*, February 9, 1998, p. 68.

Ehrenreich, Barbara, and Deirdre English. *For Her Own Good: 150 Years of the Experts' Advice to Women*. New York: Doubleday, Anchor Books, 1978.

Eisler, Riane. *The Chalice and the Blade: Our History, Our Future*. San Francisco: HarperSanFrancisco, 1987.

Elkind, David. *The Child and Society: Essays in Applied Child Development*. New York: Oxford University Press, 1979.

————. *Child Development and Education: A Piagetian Perspective*. New York: Oxford University Press, 1976.

————. "Egocentrism in Adolescence." *Child Development* 38 (1967), pp. 1025–34.

Epstein, Mark. *Going to Pieces Without Falling Apart: A Buddhist Perspective on Wholeness*. New York: Broadway Books, 1998.

————. *Thoughts Without a Thinker: Psychotherapy from a Buddhist Perspective*. New York: Basic Books, 1995.

Erikson, Erik. *Childhood and Society*. New York: W. W. Norton, 1950.

————. *Identity and the Life Cycle*. New York: W. W. Norton, 1980.

Eyer, Diane. *Motherguilt: How Our Culture Blames Mothers for What's Wrong with Society*. New York: Times Books, 1996.

Fagot, B. I., and R. Hagan. "Observations of Parent Reactions to Sex-Stereotyped Behaviors: Age and Sex Effects." *Child Development* 62, no. 3 (1991), pp. 617–628.

Fairbairn, W. Ronald. *An Object Relations Theory of the Personality*. New York: Basic Books, 1954.

————. *Psychoanalytic Studies of the Personality*. Boston: Routledge and Kegan Paul, 1952.

Faludi, Susan. *Backlash: The Undeclared War Against American Women*. New York: Crown, 1991.

Field, Tiffany. "Attachment and Separation in Young Children." *Annual Review of Psychology* 47 (1996), pp. 541–561.

Firestone, Shulamith. *The Dialectic of Sex*. New York: William Morrow, 1970.

Fort Military Information Command Center. Web site at http://www.fortmicc.com/pages/FMAR108.htm.

Fraser, Laura. *Losing It: America's Obsession with Weight and the Diet Industry That Feeds on It*. New York: E. P. Dutton, 1997.

Freeman, Lucy, and Herbert S. Strean. *Freud and Women*. New York: Frederick Ungar, 1981.

Freud, Sigmund. "Some Psychical Consequences of the Anatomical Distinction Between the Sexes." 1925. In *Standard Edition of the Complete Works of Sigmund Freud*, ed. James Strachey. Vol. 9. London: Hogarth Press, 1961.

Friedan, Betty. *The Feminine Mystique*. New York: W. W. Norton, 1963.

Frymer-Kensky, Tikva. *In the Wake of the Goddesses: Women, Culture, and the Biblical Transformation of Pagan Myth*. New York: Free Press, 1992.

Furth, Hans G. *Knowledge as Desire: An Essay on Freud and Piaget*. New York: Columbia University Press, 1987.

Gilligan, Carol. "For Many Women, Gazing at Diana Was Gazing Within." *New York Times*, September 9, 1997.

———. *In a Different Voice: Psychological Theory and Women's Development*. Cambridge, Mass.: Harvard University Press, 1982.

———. "The Riddle of Femininity and the Psychology of Love." In *Passionate Attachments: Thinking About Love*, ed. Willard Gaylin and Ethel Person. New York: Free Press, 1988.

Gimbutas, Marija. *The Civilization of the Goddess: The World of Old Europe*. San Francisco: HarperSanFrancisco, 1991.

———. *The Goddesses and Gods of Old Europe: 6500–3500 B.C.: Myths and Cult Images*. Berkeley and Los Angeles: University of California Press, 1982.

———. *The Language of the Goddess: Unearthing the Hidden Symbols of Western Civilization*. San Francisco: HarperSanFrancisco, 1989.

Goldin, Barbara Diamond. "Coming of Age in Judaism." *New Moon: The Magazine for Girls and Their Dreams* 5, no. 5 (1998), pp. 20–21.

Goleman, Daniel. *Emotional Intelligence: Why It Can Matter More Than IQ*. New York: Bantam Books, 1995.

Granrose, Cherlyn Skromme, and Eileen E. Kaplan. *Work-Family Role Choices for Women in Their Twenties and Thirties: From College Plans to Life Experiences*. Westport, Conn.: Greenwood, Praeger, 1996.

Grant, Michael. *Myths of the Greeks and the Romans*. New York: New American Library, Mentor, 1962.

Gray, John. *Men Are from Mars, Women Are from Venus: A Practical Guide for Improving Communication and Getting What You Want in Your Relationships*. New York: HarperCollins, 1992.

Grogan, Sarah, Zoe Williams, and Mark Conner. "The Effects of Viewing Same-Gender Photographic Models on Body-Esteem." *Psychology of Women Quarterly* 20, no. 4 (1996), pp. 569–575.

Gross, Michael. *Model: The Ugly Business of Beautiful Women*. New York: Warner Books, 1996.

Gross, Rita M. *Buddhism After Patriarchy*. New York: State University of New York Press, 1993.

Grosskopf, Dianne. *Sex and the Married Woman*. New York: Simon and Schuster, 1983.

Grosz, E. A. *Jacques Lacan: A Feminist Introduction*. London: Routledge, 1990.

Gustafson-Larson, Ann M., and Rhonda Dale Terry. "Weight-Related Behaviors and Concerns of Fourth-Grade Children." *Journal of the American Dietetic Association* 92 (1992), pp. 818–822.

Halifax, Joan. "The Great Matter of Life and Death." *Tricycle: The Buddhist Review* 7, no. 1 (1997), p. 20.

Harris, Judith Rich. *The Nurture Assumption: Why Children Turn Out the Way They Do*. New York: Free Press, 1998.

Heights, Roslyn. "The Influence of Fashion Magazines on the Body Image Satisfaction of College Women: An Exploratory Analysis." *Adolescence* 32, no. 127 (1997), pp. 603–614.

Hertz, Rosanna. *More Equal Than Others: Women and Men in Dual-Career Marriages*. Berkeley and Los Angeles: University of California Press, 1986.

Hesiod. *The Works and the Days; Theogony; The Shield of Herakles*. Trans. Richmond Lattimore. Ann Arbor: University of Michigan Press, 1959.

Heyn, Dalma. *The Erotic Silence of the American Wife*. New York: Random House, 1992.

Hite, Shere. *The Hite Report*. New York: Macmillan, 1976.

Hochschild, Arlie P. *The Second Shift: Working Parents and the Revolution at Home*. New York: Viking, 1989.

Hunt, Mary E. "It's Inevitable: Women Will Be Ordained." *National Catholic Reporter*, February 22, 1997.

————. "Psychological Implications of Women's Spiritual Health." *Women and Therapy* 16, nos. 2–3 (1995), pp. 21–32.

Hurlbert, David Farley, and Carol Apt. "Female Sexual Desire, Response, and Behavior." *Behavior Modification* 18, no. 4 (1994), pp. 488–504.

————. "Female Sexuality: A Comparative Study Between Women in Homosexual and Heterosexual Relationships." *Journal of Sex and Marital Therapy* 19, no. 4 (1993), pp. 315–327.

Hurlbert, David Farley, Carol Apt, and Sarah Meyers Rabehl. "Key Variables to Understanding Female Sexual Satisfaction: An Examination of Women in Nondistressed Marriages." *Journal of Sex and Marital Therapy* 19, no. 2 (1993), pp. 154–165.

Hurlbert, David Farley, and Karen Elizabeth Whittaker. "The Role of Masturbation in Marital and Sexual Satisfaction: A Comparative Study of Female Masturbators and Nonmasturbators." *Journal of Sex Education and Therapy* 17, no. 4 (1991), pp. 272–282.

Jung, Carl G. *The Collected Works* (Bollingen Series 20, 20 vols.). Trans. R. F. C. Hull and ed. H. Read, M. Fordham, G. Adler, and W. McGuire. Princeton, N.J.: Princeton University Press, 1953–1979.

————. *The Collected Works of C. G. Jung: The Archetypes and the Collective Unconscious*. 2d ed. Vol. 9, pt. 1. Trans. R. F. C. Hull. Princeton, N.J.: Princeton University Press, 1969.

————. *The Collected Works of C. G. Jung: Experimental Researches*. Vol. 2. Trans. L. Stein. Princeton, N.J.: Princeton University Press, 1973.

————. *The Collected Works of C. G. Jung: The Structure and Dynamics of the Psyche*. 2d ed. Vol. 8. Trans. R. F. C. Hull. Princeton, N.J.: Princeton University Press, 1969.

————. *Letters: 1906–1950*. Vol. 1. Trans. R. F. C. Hull and ed. G. Adler. Princeton, N.J.: Princeton University Press, 1973.

————. *Psychology and Religion*. New Haven, Conn.: Yale University Press, 1938.

Kernberg, Otto. *Love Relations: Normality and Pathology*. New Haven, Conn.: Yale University Press, 1995.

Klein, Anne Carolyn. *Meeting the Great Bliss Queen: Buddhists, Feminists, and the Art of Self*. Boston: Beacon Press, 1995.

Klemchuk, Helen P., Cheryl B. Hutchinson, and Rochelle I. Frank. "Body Dissatisfaction and Eating-Related Problems on the College Campus: Usefulness of the Eating Disorder Inventory with a Nonclinical Population." *Journal of Counseling Psychology* 37, no. 3 (1990), pp. 297–305.

Klemke, Lloyd. *The Sociology of Shoplifting: Boosters and Snitchers Today*. New York: Praeger, 1992.

Kowalski, R. M. "Inferring Sexual Interest from Behavioral Clues: Effects, Gender, and Sexually Relevant Attitudes." *Sex Roles* 29 (1993), pp. 13–36.

Le Blanc, A. N. "Harassment in the Hall." *Seventeen*, September 1992, pp. 163–165.

Le Doux, James. *The Emotional Brain: The Mysterious Underpinnings of Emotional Life*. New York: Simon and Schuster, 1996.

Lejoyeux, Michel, Jean Adès, Valérie Tassain, and Jacquelyn Solomon. "Phenomenology and Psychopathology of Uncontrolled Buying." *American Journal of Psychiatry* 153, no. 12 (December 1996), pp. 1524–29.

Lejoyeux, Michel, Valérie Tassain, Jacquelyn Solomon, and Jean Adès. "Study of Compulsive Buying in Depressed Patients." *Journal of Clinical Psychiatry* 58 (1997), pp. 169–173.

Lewis, Michael. "Self-Conscious Emotions and the Development of Self." *Journal of the American Psychoanalytic Association* 39, supp. (1991), pp. 45–73.

———. *Shame: The Exposed Self*. New York: Free Press, 1995.

Lifton, Robert Jay. *The Broken Connection: On Death and the Continuity of Life*. New York: Basic Books, 1979.

Louis Harris and Associates. *Hostile Hallways: The AAUW Survey on Sexual Harassment in America's Schools*. Washington, D.C.: American Association of University Women, 1993.

Macy, Joanna. *World as Lover, World as Self*. Berkeley: Parallax Press, 1991.

Mahler, Margaret S., Fred Pine, and Anni Bergman. *The Psychological Birth of the Human Infant: Symbiosis and Individuation*. New York: Basic Books, 1975.

Main, Mary. "Discourse, Prediction, and Recent Studies in Attachment: Implications for Psychoanalysis." In *Research in Psychoanalysis: Process, Development, Outcome*, ed. Theodore Shapiro and Robert N. Emde. Madison, Conn.: International Universities Press, 1995.

————. "Exploration, Play, and Cognitive Functioning Related to Infant-Mother Attachment." *Infant Behavior and Development* 6, no. 2 (1983), pp. 167–174.

————. "Recent Studies in Attachment: Overview, with Selected Implications for Clinical Work." In *Attachment Theory: Social, Developmental, and Clinical Perspectives*, ed. Susan Goldberg, Roy Muir, and John Kerr. Hillsdale, N.J.: Analytic Press, 1995.

Mairs, Nancy. *Ordinary Time: Cycles in Marriage, Faith, and Renewal*. Boston: Beacon Press, 1993.

Maltz, Wendy, and Suzie Boss. *In the Garden of Desire: The Intimate World of Women's Sexual Fantasies*. New York: Broadway Books, 1997.

Michael, Robert T., John H. Gagnon, Edward O. Laumann, and Gina Kolata. *Sex in America: A Definitive Survey*. Boston and New York: Little, Brown, 1994.

Millman, Marcia. *Warm Hearts and Cold Cash: The Intimate Dynamics of Families and Money*. New York: Free Press, 1991.

Mintz, Laurie B., and Nancy E. Betz. "Prevalence and Correlates of Eating Disordered Behaviors Among Undergraduate Women." *Journal of Counseling Psychology* 35, no. 4 (1988), pp. 463–471.

Mitchell, Juliet, and Jacqueline Rose, eds. *Feminine Sexuality: Jacques Lacan and the Ecole Freudienne*. Trans. Jacqueline Rose. New York: W. W. Norton, 1982.

Moen, Phyllis. *Women's Two Roles: A Contemporary Dilemma*. Westport, Conn.: Auburn House, 1992.

Morton, Andrew. *Diana: Her New Life*. New York: Simon and Schuster, 1994.

Myers, Philip N., Jr. "The Elastic Body Image: The Effect of Television Advertising and Programming on Body Image Distortions in Young

Women." *Journal of Communication* 42, no. 3 (Summer 1992), pp. 108–133.

Nathanson, Daniel L., ed. *The Many Faces of Shame*. New York: Guilford Press, 1987.

National Institute of Child Health and Human Development, Early Child Care Research Network. "The Effects of Infant Child Care on Infant-Mother Attachment Security: Results of the NICHD Study of Early Child Care." *Child Development* 68, no. 5 (1997), pp. 860–879.

Neumann, Erich. *The Child*. Boston: Shambhala, 1990.

Newman, Judith. "Little Girls Who Won't Eat: The Alarming Epidemic of Eating Disorders." *Redbook*, October 1997, pp. 120–154.

Oliver, Mary. *New and Selected Poems*. Boston: Beacon Press, 1992.

Overton, W. F. *Reasoning, Necessity, and Logic: Developmental Perspectives*. Hillsdale, N.J.: Lawrence Erlbaum, 1990.

Peters, Joan. *When Mothers Work: Loving Our Children Without Sacrificing Our Selves*. Reading, Mass.: Addison-Wesley, 1997.

Petersen, Anne C., P. A. Sarigiani, and R. E. Kennedy. "Adolescent Depression: Why More Girls?" *Journal of Youth and Adolescence* 20, no. 2 (1991), pp. 247–271.

Phelps, Ethel Johnston, ed. *The Maid of the North: Feminist Folk Tales from Around the World*. New York: Holt, Rinehart, and Winston, 1981.

Piaget, Jean. *The Language and Thought of the Child*. Trans. M. Warden. New York: Harcourt, Brace, 1926.

Pipher, Mary. *Reviving Ophelia: Saving the Lives of Adolescent Girls*. New York: G. P. Putnam's Sons, 1994.

Plaskow, Judith, and Carol P. Christ, eds. *Weaving the Visions: New Patterns in Feminist Spirituality*. San Francisco: HarperSanFrancisco, 1989.

Polivy, Janet, D. M. Garner, and P. E. Garfinkel. "Causes and Consequences of the Current Preference for Thin Female Physiques." In *Physical Appearance, Stigma, and Social Behavior: The Ontario Symposium*, ed. C. P. Herman, M. P. Zanna, and E. T. Higgins. Vol. 3. Hillsdale, N.J.: Lawrence Erlbaum, 1986.

Reinisch, June M. *The Kinsey Institute New Report on Sex: What You Must Know to Be Sexually Literate*. New York: St. Martin's Press, 1990.

Rich, Adrienne. *Of Woman Born: Motherhood as Experience and Institution*. New York: W. W. Norton, 1976.

Rosen, Raymond C., Jennifer B. Taylor, Sandra R. Leiblum, and Gloria A. Bachmann. "Prevalence of Sexual Dysfunction in Women: Results of a Survey Study of 329 Women in an Outpatient Gynecological Clinic." *Journal of Sex and Marital Therapy* 19, no. 3 (1993), pp. 171–188.

Rozin, Paul, and April E. Fallon. "Body Images, Attitudes to Weight, and Misperceptions of Figure Preferences of the Opposite Sex: A Comparison of Men and Women in Two Generations." *Journal of Abnormal Psychology* 97, no. 3 (1988), pp. 342–345.

Russell, Jeanie. "Klepto Nation." *Allure*, February 1998, pp. 129–131, 151.

Sadker, Myra, and David Sadker. *Failing at Fairness: How America's Schools Cheat Girls*. New York: Macmillan, 1994.

Sands, Donald. "The Marriage of Sir Gawain and the Lady Ragnell." In *Middle English Verse Romances*. New York: Holt, Rinehart, and Winston, 1966.

Schlosser, Steven, Donald W. Black, Susan Repertinger, and Daniel Freet. "Compulsive Buying: Demography, Phenomenology, and Comorbidity in Forty-six Subjects." *General Hospital Psychiatry* 16 (1994), pp. 205–212.

Schneiderman, Stuart. *Jacques Lacan: The Death of an Intellectual Hero*. Cambridge, Mass.: Harvard University Press, 1983.

Secret, Mary, and Robert G. Green. "Occupational Status Differences Among Three Groups of Married Mothers." *Affilia* 13, no. 1 (1998), pp. 47–68.

Siegel, Rachel Josefowitz. "'I Don't Know Enough': Jewish Women's Learned Ignorance." In *Celebrating the Lives of Jewish Women*, ed. Rachel Josefowitz Siegel and Ellen Cole. New York: Haworth Press, 1997.

Smith, Joseph H., and William Kerrigan, eds. *Interpreting Lacan: Psychiatry and the Humanities*. Vol. 6. New Haven, Conn.: Yale University Press, 1983.

Spitz, Rene A. *The First Year of Life: A Psychoanalytic Study of Normal and Deviant Development of Object Relations*. New York: International Universities Press, 1965.

Spoto, Donald. *Diana: The Last Year.* New York: Harmony Books, 1997.

Spretnak, Charlene. *States of Grace: The Recovery of Meaning in the Postmodern Age.* San Francisco: HarperCollins, 1991.

——, ed. *The Politics of Women's Spirituality: Essays by Founding Mothers of the Movement.* New York: Anchor Books, 1994.

Starhawk. *Dreaming the Dark: Magic, Sex, and Politics.* Boston: Beacon Press, 1982.

——. *The Spiral Dance: A Rebirth of the Ancient Religion of the Great Goddess.* New York: Harper and Row, 1979.

Stern, Daniel. *The Interpersonal World of the Infant.* New York: Basic Books, 1985.

Stice, E., E. Schupak-Neuberg, H. E. Shaw, and R. I. Stein. "Relation of Media Exposure to Eating Disorder Symptomatology: An Examination of Mediating Mechanisms." *Journal of Abnormal Psychology* 103 (1994), pp. 836–840.

Stice, E., and H. E. Shaw. "Adverse Effects of the Media-Portrayed Thin-Ideal on Women and Linkages to Bulimic Symptomatology." *Journal of Social and Clinical Psychology* 13 (1994), pp. 288–308.

Suzuki, Daisetz Teitaro. *The Training of the Zen Buddhist Monk.* New York: University Books, 1959.

Symington, Neville. *Narcissism: A New Theory.* London: Karnac Books, 1997.

Tannen, Deborah. *Talking from Nine to Five: Women and Men in the Workplace: Language, Sex, and Power.* New York: William Morrow, 1994.

Tavris, Carol. *The Mismeasure of Woman.* New York: Simon and Schuster, 1992.

Taylor, Charles. *The Ethics of Authenticity.* Cambridge, Mass.: Harvard University Press, 1991.

Telushkin, Joseph. "Women Rabbis." In *Jewish Literacy: The Most Important Things to Know About the Jewish Religion, Its People, and History.* New York: William Morrow, 1991.

Thelen, Mark H., Anne H. Powell, Christine Lawrence, and Mark E. Kuhnert. "Eating and Body Image Concerns Among Children." *Journal of Clinical Child Psychology* 21, no. 1 (1992), pp. 60–69.

Thompson, J. Kevin, ed. *Body Image, Eating Disorders, and Obesity*. Washington, D.C.: American Psychological Association, 1996.

Thornton, Bill, and Jason Maurice. "Physique Contrast Effect: Adverse Impact of Idealized Body Images for Women." *Sex Roles* 37, nos. 5–6 (September 1997), pp. 433–439.

Tibbets, Stephen G., and Denise C. Hertz. "Gender Differences in Factors of Social Control and Rational Choice." *Deviant Behavior: An Interdisciplinary Journal* 17 (1996), pp. 183–208.

Torjesen, Karen Jo. *When Women Were Priests: Women's Leadership in the Early Church and the Scandal of Their Subordination in the Rise of Christianity*. San Francisco: HarperSanFrancisco, 1993.

United Church of Christ Board for Homeland Ministry, Research Department. 770 Prospect Avenue, Cleveland, Ohio, 44115. Phone: (216) 736-3813.

Waddell, L. Austine. *Tibetan Buddhism: With Its Mystic Cults, Symbolism, and Mythology*. New York: Dover, 1972.

Wehr, Demaris S. "When Good People Do Bad Things: Spiritual Abuse." In *Paths of Integrity, Wisdom, and Transcendence*, ed. Polly Young-Eisendrath and Mel Miller. In press.

"Who, What, Where, and How Do You Love?" *Redbook*, October 1989, p. 134.

Wilcox, Sara. "Age and Gender in Relation to Body Attitudes: Is There a Double Standard of Aging?" *Psychology of Women Quarterly* 21, no. 4 (1997), pp. 549–565.

Wilson, Edward O. *Sociobiology: The New Synthesis*. Cambridge, Mass.: Harvard University Press, 1975.

Winnicott, Donald W. *The Family and Individual Development*. New York: Basic Books, 1965.

———. *Mother and Child: A Primer of First Relationships*. New York: Basic Books, 1957.

Wolf, Naomi. *The Beauty Myth: How Images of Beauty Are Used Against Women*. New York: William Morrow, 1991.

———. *Promiscuities: The Secret Struggle for Womanhood*. New York: Random House, 1997.

Young-Eisendrath, Polly. *Gender and Desire: Uncursing Pandora*. College Station: Texas A & M University Press, 1997.

———. "Gender and Individuation: Relating to Self and Other." In *Mirrors of Transformation: The Self in Relationships*, ed. D. E. Brien. Berwyn, Penn.: Round Table Press, 1995, pp. 21–39.

———. *Hags and Heroes: A Feminist Approach to Jungian Psychotherapy with Couples*. Toronto: Inner City Books, 1984.

———. *You're Not What I Expected: Learning to Love the Opposite Sex*. New York: William Morrow, 1993.

Young-Eisendrath, Polly, and James A. Hall. *Jung's Self Psychology: A Constructivist Perspective*. New York: Guilford Press, 1991.

Young-Eisendrath, Polly, and Florence Wiedemann. *Female Authority: Empowering Women Through Psychotherapy*. New York: Guilford Press, 1987.

Zikmund, Barbara Brown, Adair T. Lumnis, and Patricia M. Y. Chang. "Women, Men, and Styles of Leadership." *Christian Century*, May 6, 1998, pp. 478–486.

Index

About the Author

Polly Young-Eisendrath, Ph.D., is a psychologist and Jungian psychoanalyst practicing in Burlington, Vermont. Clinical associate professor of psychiatry at the University of Vermont Medical College, she has published ten books, many chapters and articles, and she lectures widely on topics of women's development, resilience, couple relationship, and the interface of contemporary psychoanalysis and spirituality.